NATIVE AMERICAN FOLKTALES

Edited by
Thomas A. Green

Stories from the American Mosaic

GREENWOOD PRESS
Westport, Connecticut • London

Library of Congress Cataloging-in-Publication Data

Native American folktales / edited by Thomas A. Green
    p. cm. — (Stories from the American mosaic)
  Includes bibliographical references and index.
  ISBN: 978–0–313–36301–6 (alk. paper)
1. Indians of North America—Folklore. 2. Tales—United States. 3. United States—Folklore.
I. Green, Thomas A., 1944–
E98.F6N382 2009
398.20973—dc22   2008032977

British Library Cataloguing in Publication Data is available.

Library of Congress Catalog Card Number: 2008032977
ISBN-13: 978–0–313–36301–6

First published in 2009

Greenwood Press, 88 Post Road West, Westport, CT 06881
An imprint of Greenwood Publishing Group, Inc.
www.greenwood.com

Printed in the United States of America

The paper used in this book complies with the
Permanent Paper Standard issued by the National
Information Standards Organization (Z39.48-1984).

10 9 8 7 6 5 4 3 2 1

Contents

Preface

Native American Folktales is designed to provide educators, students, and general readers with examples of a range of traditional Native American narrative types: fictional tales, legends, myths, and personal experience narratives. Given the hundreds of distinct indigenous cultures in the Americas, the collection cannot be comprehensive. The volume, however, does contain representative examples of the storytelling traditions of major Native North American geographic and cultural areas: Northeast, Southeast, Southwest, Basin, California, Plains, Northwest, Sub-Arctic, and Arctic. The tales reflect the environment, cultural adaptations, and prevailing concerns of the respective areas from which they are drawn, as well as more general features of the Native American worldview. The introductions to each tale comment on these issues. The concluding general bibliography provides additional resources for those readers who wish to explore these issues in greater depth.

The collection is divided into four parts. "Origins" encompasses those narratives that focus on beginnings and transformations: the creation of the world and its inhabitants and how animal species acquired their physical characteristics, for example. "Heroes, Heroines, Villains, and Fools" presents a cross-section of major character types that populate Native American folktales. "Society and Conflict" contains considerations of social issues ranging from conventional morality to intergroup conflicts. Finally, "The Supernatural" concentrates on traditional tales of the dead, the magical, and the monstrous.

The narratives have been modified from their original forms for the benefit of contemporary readers. The modifications have been held to the minimum necessary to translate these tales for their intended audiences, to eliminate redundancy in some cases, and, in a few cases, alternative terminology has been substituted for terms (particularly racially charged terms) that would prove offensive to contemporary readers. The source of each selection is noted at its conclusion for the benefit of readers who wish to read the original texts.

ORIGINS

The Hopi Creation of the World

The Hopi established a village culture in what is now Arizona. The creation myths they recount vary from clan to clan. This particular narrative focuses on a pair of themes: the creation of life forms by a pair of female deities and the introduction of strife into the world by Spider Woman, a common agent of turmoil in Hopi traditional tales. The presence of Spaniards in this myth marks it as a relatively modern creation.

A very long time ago there was nothing but water. In the east, Stone Woman, the deity of all hard substances, lived in the ocean. Her house was a kiva (ceremonial chamber entered from an opening in the ceiling) like the kivas of the Hopi of today. To the ladder leading into the kiva were usually tied a skin of a gray fox and one of a yellow fox. Another Stone Woman lived in the ocean in the west in a similar kiva, but to her ladder was attached a turtle-shell rattle.

The Sun also existed at that time. Shortly before rising in the east the Sun would dress up in the skin of the gray fox, whereupon it would begin to dawn—the so-called white dawn of the Hopi. After a little while the Sun would lay off the gray skin and put on the yellow fox skin, whereupon the bright dawn of the morning—the so-called yellow dawn of the Hopi—would appear. The Sun would then rise, that is, emerge from an opening in the north end of the kiva in which Stone Woman lived. When arriving in the west again, the Sun would first announce his arrival by fastening the rattle on the point of the ladder beam, whereupon he would enter the kiva, pass through an opening in the north end of the kiva, and continue his course eastward under the water and so on.

By and by these two deities caused some dry land to appear in the midst of the water, the waters receding eastward and westward. The Sun passing over this dry land constantly took notice of the fact, that no living being of any kind could be seen anywhere, and mentioned this fact to the two deities. So one time the Stone Woman of the west sent word through the Sun to the Stone Woman in the east to come over to her as she wanted to talk over this matter. The Stone Woman of the east complied with this request and proceeded to the west over a rainbow.

After consulting each other on this point the two concluded that they would create a little bird; so the deity of the east made a wren of clay, and covered it up with a piece of woven cloth. Hereupon they sang a song over it, and after a little while the little bird showed signs of life.

Uncovering it, a live bird came forth, saying, "Why do you want me so quickly?"

"Yes," they said, "we want you to fly all over this dry place and see whether you can find anything living." They thought that as the Sun always passed over the middle of the earth, he might have failed to notice any living beings that might exist in the north or the south. So the little wren, flew all over the earth, but upon its return reported that no living being existed anywhere. Tradition says, however, that by this time Spider Woman, lived somewhere in the southwest at the edge of the water, also in a kiva, but this the little bird had failed to notice.

Hereupon the deity of the west proceeded to make very many birds of different kinds and forms, placing them again under the same cover under which the wren had been brought to life. They again sang a song over them. Presently the birds began to move under the cover. The goddess removed the cover and found under it all kinds of birds and fowls. "Why do you want us so quickly?" the latter asked.

"Yes, we want you to inhabit this world." Hereupon the two deities taught every kind of bird the sound that it should make, and then the birds scattered out in all directions.

Hereupon the Stone Woman of the west made of clay all different kinds of animals, and they were brought to life in the same manner as the birds. They also asked the same question, "Why do you want us so quickly?"

"We want you to inhabit this earth," was the reply given to them, whereupon they were taught by their creators their different sounds or languages, after which they proceeded forth to inhabit the different parts of the earth. They concluded that they would create man. The deity of the east made of clay first a woman and then a man, who were brought to life in exactly the same manner as the birds and animals before them. They asked the same question, and were told that they should live upon this earth and should understand everything.

Hereupon the Stone Woman of the east made two tablets of some hard substance, whether stone or clay our history does not say, and drew upon them with the wooden stick certain characters, handing these tablets to the newly created man and woman, who looked at them, but did not know what they meant. So the deity of the east rubbed with the palms of her hands, first the palms of the woman and then the palms of the man, by which they were enlightened so that they understood the writing on the tablets.

Hereupon the deities taught these two a language. After they had taught them the language, the goddess of the east took them out of the kiva and led them over a rainbow, to her home in the east. There they stayed for four days, after which Eastern Stone Woman told them to go and select for themselves a place and live there. The two proceeded forth saying that they would travel around awhile and wherever they would find a good field they would remain. Finding a nice place at last, they built a small, simple house, similar to the old houses of the Hopi.

Soon the Stone Woman of the west began to think of the matter again, and said to herself, "This is not the way yet that it should be. We are not done yet," and communicated her thoughts to the Stone Woman of the east.

By this time Spider Woman had heard about all this matter and she concluded to anticipate others and therefore, also create some beings. So she also made a man and woman of clay, covered them up, sang over them, and brought to life her handiwork. But these two proved to be Spaniards. She taught them the Spanish language, also giving them similar tablets and imparting knowledge to them by rubbing their hands in the same manner as the woman of the East had done with the "White Men." Hereupon she created two burros, which she gave to the Spanish man and woman. The latter settled down close by. After this, Spider Woman continued to create people in the same manner as she had created the Spaniards, always a man and a woman, giving a different language to each pair. But all at once she found that she had forgotten to create a woman for a certain man; and that is the reason why now there are always some single men.

She continued the creating of people in the same manner, giving new languages as the pairs were formed. All at once she found that she had failed to create a man for a certain woman, in other words, it was found that there was one woman more than there were men. "Oh my!" she said, "How is this?" and then addressing the single woman she said: "There is a single man somewhere, who went away from here. You try to find him and if he accepts you, you live with him. If not, both of you will have to remain single. You do the best you can about that."

The two finally found each other, and the woman said, "Where shall we live?" The man answered: "Why here, anywhere. We shall remain together." So he went to work and built a house for them to live in. But it did not take very long before they commenced to quarrel with each other. "I want to live here alone," the woman said. "I can prepare food for myself." "Yes, but who will get the wood for you? Who will work the fields?" the man said. "We had better remain together." They made up with each other, but peace did not last. They soon quarreled again, separated for a while, and came together again, separated again, and so on. Had these people not lived in that way, all the other Hopi would now live in peace, but others learned it from them, and that is the reason why there are so many contentions between the men and their wives. These were the kind of people that Spider Woman had created.

The Stone Woman of the west heard about this and commenced to medi-
tate upon it. Soon she called the goddess from the east to come over again,
which the latter did. "I do not want to live here alone," the deity of the west
said, "I also want some good people to live here." So she also created a
number of other people, but always a man and a wife. They were created
in the same manner as the deity of the east had created hers. They lived in
the west. Only wherever the people that Spider Woman had created came
in contact with these good people there was trouble.

The people at that time led a wandering life, living mostly on game. Wherever they found rabbits, antelopes, or deer they killed the game and ate it.
This led to a good many contentions among the people. Finally the Woman
of the west said to her people: "You remain here; I am going to live, after
this, in the midst of the ocean in the west. When you want anything from
me, you pray to me there." Her people regretted this very much, but she left
them. The Stone Woman of the east did exactly the same thing, and that is
the reason why at the present day the places where these two live are
never seen.

Those Hopi who want something from them deposit their prayer offerings
in the village. When they say their wishes and prayers they think of those
two who live in the far distance, but the Hopi believe that the deities still
remember them.

The Spanish were angry at Stone Woman and two of them took their guns
and proceeded to the abiding place of the deity. The Spaniards are very skillful, and they found a way to get there. When they arrived at the house of
Stone Woman the latter at once surmised what their intentions were. "You
have come to kill me," she said; "don't do that; lay down your weapons
and I shall show you something; I am not going to hurt you." They laid
down their arms, whereupon she went to the rear end of the kiva and
brought out a white lump, like a stone, and laid it before the two men,
asking them to lift it up.

One tried it, but could not lift it up, and what was worse, his hands
adhered to the stone. The other man tried to assist him, but his hands also
adhered to the stone, and thus they were both prisoners. Hereupon Stone
Woman took the two guns and said, "These do not amount to anything,"
and then rubbed them between her hands to powder.

She then said to them: "You people ought to live in peace with one
another. You people of Spider Woman know many things, and the people
whom we have made also know many, but different, things. You ought
not to quarrel about these things, but learn from one another; if one has or
knows a good thing he should exchange it with others for other good things
that they know and have. If you will agree to this I shall release you. They
said they did, and that they would no more try to kill the deity. Then the
goddess went to the rear end of the kiva where she disappeared through an
opening in the floor, from where she exerted a secret influence upon the

stone and thus released the two men, They departed, but Stone Woman did not fully trust them, thinking that they would return, but they never did.

Source: Adapted from "The Origin," H.R. Voth, *The Traditions of the Hopi.* Field Columbian Museum, Publication 96. (Chicago: Field Columbian Museum, 1905), pp. 1–5.

Raven Befriends the Human Race

Whether cast as benefactor or rogue, Raven is a central figure in the mythology of Native American cultures from the northwest coast of the United States to Arctic Canada. In this Inuit (Eskimo) myth of the first humans, Raven befriends the first men who emerge from pods of a giant pea pod. He creates women for companionship, animals and plants to provide the raw materials for survival, and fire, tools, and shelter to allow humanity to adapt to the harsh environment. While a culture hero and not truly a Creator, Raven can be seen as an important secondary figure who transforms the world to serve Inuit needs.

In the time before there were any people on earth, a large pea-vine was growing on the beach, and in the pod of this pea the first man lay coiled up for four days. On the fifth day he stretched out his feet and that made the pod burst. He fell to the ground, where he stood up—a full-grown man.

He had never seen anything that looked like him, and he did not know what to make of himself. He looked around, and then at himself; then he moved his arms and hands and was surprised that he could do it. He moved his neck and his legs, and examined himself curiously.

Looking back, he saw the pod from which he had fallen still attached to the vine, with a hole at the lower end out of which he had dropped. He went up and looked in through the hole to see if there were any more like him in the pod. Then he looked about him again, and saw that he was getting farther away from the place where he started, and that the ground seemed very soft and moved up and down under his feet.

After a while he had an unpleasant feeling in his stomach, and stooped down to take water in his mouth from a small pool at his feet. The water ran down into his stomach and he felt better. When he looked up again, he saw a big dark object coming through the air with a waving motion. It came on until it was just in front of him when it stopped and, standing on the ground, looked at him.

This was Raven, and as soon as it stopped it raised one of its wings, pushed up its beak like a mask, to the top of its head, and changed at once into a man. Before he raised his mask, the Raven had stared at the Man, and later he stared more than ever, moving about from side to side to obtain a better view. At last he said, "What are you? Where did you come from? I have never seen anything like you."

He looked again and said, "You are so much like me in shape that you surprise me."

Next, he said, "Walk away a few steps so that I may see you more clearly. I am astonished at you! I have never before seen anything like you. Where did you come from?"

"I came from the pea-pod," said Man pointing to the plant from which he came.

"Ah!" exclaimed Raven, I made that vine, but did not know that anything like you would ever come out of it. Come with me to the high ground over there. This ground I made later and it is still soft and thin, but it is harder and thicker over there." They came to the higher ground which was firm under their feet.

"Have you eaten anything?" Raven asked Man.

"I took some soft stuff into me at one of the pools," replied Man.

"Ah! You drank water," said Raven. "Now wait for me here."

He drew down the mask over his face, changing again into a bird, and flew far up into the sky where he disappeared. Man waited where he had been left until the fourth day, when Raven returned, bringing four berries. Pushing up his mask, Raven became a man again and held out two salmon berries and two heath berries.

"Here is what I made for you to eat. I wish them to be plentiful over the earth. Now eat them."

Man took the berries and placed them in his mouth one after the other, and they satisfied his hunger, which had made him feel uncomfortable. Raven then led Man to a small creek near by and left him till he went to the edge of the water and molded two pieces of clay into the form of a pair of mountain sheep. He held them in his hand until they were dry and then called Man to show him what he had done.

"Those are very pretty," said Man.

"Close your eyes for a little while," said Raven. As soon as Man's eyes were closed Raven drew down his mask and waved his wings four times over the images, when they came to life and bounded away as full-grown mountain sheep.

Raven then raised his mask and said, "Look! Look quick!" When Man saw the sheep moving away full of life he cried out with pleasure.

Seeing how pleased he was, Raven said, "If these animals are numerous, perhaps people will wish very much to get them."

"I think they will," said Man.

"Well, it will be better for them to have their home in the high cliffs," said Raven, and only there shall they be found, so that everyone cannot kill them."

Then Raven made two animals of clay and gave them life when they were dry only in spots, and they remained brown and white and were the tame reindeer with mottled coats.

"Those are very handsome," exclaimed Man, admiring them.

"Yes, but there will not be many of these," said Raven.

Then he made a pair of wild reindeer and let them get dry only on their bellies before giving them life; and to this day the belly of the wild reindeer is the only white part about it.

"These animals will be very common and people will kill many of them," said Raven.

"You will be very lonely by yourself," said Raven to Man one day. "I will make you a companion." He went to a spot some distance from where he had made the animals, and, looking now and then at Man as an artist looks at his model, he made an image very much like Man. He took from the creek some fine water grass and fastened it on the back of the head for hair. After the image had dried in his hands, he waved his wings as he had done with all the live things, and the image came to life and stood beside Man, a beautiful young woman.

"There is a companion for you!" cried Raven. "Now come with me to this knoll over here."

In those days there were no mountains far or near, and the sun never ceased to shine brightly. No rain ever fell, and no winds blew. When they came to the knoll Raven found a patch of long, dry moss and showed the pair how to make a bed in it, and they slept very warmly.

Raven drew down his mask and slept near by in the form of a bird. Wakening before the others, Raven went to the creek and made three pairs of fishes: sticklebacks, graylings, and blackfish. When they were swimming about in the water, he called to Man, "Come and see what I have made."

When Man saw the sticklebacks swimming up the stream with a wriggling motion, he was so surprised that he raised his hands suddenly and the fish darted away.

"Look at these graylings," said Raven; "they will be found in clear mountain streams, while the sticklebacks are already on their way to the sea. Both are good for food; so, whether you live beside the water or in the upland, you may find plenty to eat."

He looked about and thought there was nothing on the land as lively as the fish in the water, so he made the shrew-mice, for he said, "They will skip about and enliven the ground and prevent it from looking dead and barren, even if they are not good for food."

For several days he kept making other animals, more fishes, and a few ground birds, for as yet there were no trees for birds to alight in. Every time he made anything he explained to Man what it was and what it would do.

After this he flew away to the sky and was gone four days, when he returned bringing a salmon for Man and his wife. He thought that the ponds and lakes seemed silent and lonely, so he made insects to fly over their surfaces, and muskrats and beavers to swim about near their borders. At that time the mosquito did not bite as it does now, and he said to Man, "I made these flying creatures to enliven the world and make it cheerful. The skin of this muskrat you are to use for clothing. The beaver is very cunning and only good hunters can catch it. It will live in the streams and build strong houses, and you must follow its example and build a house."

When a child was born, Raven and Man took it to the creek and rubbed it with clay, and carried it back to the stopping-place on the knoll. The next morning the child was running about pulling up grass and other plants, which Raven had caused to grow near by. On the third day the child became a full-grown man.

Raven one day went to the creek and made a bear, and gave it life; but he jumped aside very quickly when the bear stood up and looked fiercely about. He had thought there ought to be some animal of which Man would be afraid, and now he was almost afraid of the bear himself.

"You would better keep away from that animal," he said. "It is very fierce and will tear you to pieces if you disturb it."

He made various kinds of seals, and said to Man, "You are to eat these and to take their skins for clothing. Cut some of the skins into strips and make snares to catch deer. But you must not snare deer yet; wait until they are more numerous."

By and by another child was born, this time a girl, and the Man and Woman rubbed it with clay as Raven had taught them to do, and the next day the little girl walked about. On the third day she was a full-grown woman, for in those days people grew up very fast, so that the earth would be peopled.

Raven went back to the pea-vine and there he found that three other men had just fallen from the pod, out of which the first one had dropped. These men, like the first, were looking about in wonder not knowing what to make of themselves and the world about them.

"Come with me," said Raven; and he led them away in an opposite direction from the one in which he had led the first Man, and brought them to solid land close to the sea. "Stop here, and I will teach you what to do and how to live," said he.

He caused some small trees and bushes to grow on the hillside and in the hollows, and he took a piece of wood from one of these, and a cord, and made a bow and showed them how to shoot game for food. Then he taught them to make fire with a fire-drill. He made plants, and gulls, and loons, and other birds such as to fly about on the seacoast.

Then he made three clay images somewhat resembling the men, and waved his wings over them and brought them to life as women, and led each one of these women to one of the men, and then led each pair to a dry bank, and had three families started on three hilltops.

"Go down to the shore," he said to the three men and the three women, "and bring up the logs that the tide has brought in, and I will show you how to make houses."

They brought the drift logs, and he showed them how to lay them up for walls, and how to make a roof of branches covered with earth. Seals had now become numerous, and he taught them how to capture them, and what use to make of their skins. He helped them to make arrows and spears, and nets to capture deer and fish, and other implements of the chase. He showed them how to make kayaks by stretching green hides over a framework of ribs, and letting the hides dry.

"I have not made as many birds and animals for you as I made for First Man and his wife, but I have made you so many more plants and trees that it isn't quite fair to him. I must go back and fix up his land a bit," said Raven.

So he went over to where First Man and his wife and children were living, and told them all he had done for the three men who had come out of the pea-pod, and how well he had them fixed up.

"I must have you live as well as they do," he said. "Your land looks rather barren, and you have no houses."

That night while the people slept he caused birch, spruce, and cottonwood trees to spring up in the low places, and when the people awoke in the morning they clapped their hands in delight, for the birds were singing in the tree-tops, and the green leaves with the sunlight flickering through them made it seem like a fairy land. And they were delighted with the shade of the trees in which they could sit and watch the quivering lights and shadows, which the fluttering of the leaves made.

Then Raven taught these people how to build houses out of the trees and bushes, and how to make fire with a fire-drill and to place the spark of tinder in a bunch of dry grass and wave it about until it blazed, and then put dry wood upon it. He showed them how to put a stick through their fish and hold it in the fire, till it was a thousand times more delicious than when raw. He took willow twigs and strips of willow bark, and made traps for catching fish; and, best of all, taught them to look out for the future, by catching more salmon than they needed, when salmon were running, and drying them for use when they could catch none.

Source: Adapted from "The First Man, The First Woman, and Other People," Clara K. Bayliss, *A Treasury of Eskimo Tales.* (New York: Thomas Y. Crowell Company, 1922), pp. 52–64.

The First Fire

The acquisition of fire plays a pivotal role in the origin myths of all cultures. Beyond it's obvious functions, fire symbolizes technology in its broadest sense. The following Cherokee narrative serves the additional function of explaining how the animals who set about to obtain fire acquired their distinctive attributes.

In the beginning there was no fire, and the world was cold, until the Thunders, who lived up beyond the arch of the sky, sent their lightning and put fire into the bottom of a hollow sycamore tree that grew on an island. The animals knew it was there, because they could see the smoke coming out at the top, but they could not get to it on account of the water that lay between them and the island, so they held a council to decide what to do. This was a long time ago.

Every animal that could fly or swim was anxious to go after the fire. The Raven offered, and because he was so large and strong they thought he could surely do the work, so he was sent first. He flew high and far across the water and alighted on the sycamore tree, but while he was wondering what to do next, the heat had scorched all his feathers black, and he was frightened and came back without the fire. The little Screech-owl volunteered to go, and reached the place safely, but while he was looking down into the hollow tree a blast of hot air came up and nearly burned out his eyes. He managed to fly home as best he could, but it was a long time before he could see well, and his eyes are red to this day. Then the Hooting Owl and the Horned Owl went, but by the time they got to the hollow tree the fire was burning so fiercely that the smoke nearly blinded them, and the ashes carried up by the wind made white rings about their eyes. They had to come home again without the fire, but with all their rubbing they were never able to get rid of the white rings.

No more of the birds would venture, and so the little snake, the black racer, said he would go through the water and bring back some fire. He swam across to the island and crawled through the grass to the tree, and went in by a small hole at the bottom. The heat and smoke were too much for him, too, and after dodging about blindly over the hot ashes until he was almost on fire himself he managed by good luck to get out again at the same hole, but his body had been scorched black, and he has ever since had the habit of darting and doubling on his track as if trying to escape from close quarters. He came back, and the great blacksnake, "The Climber," offered to go for fire. He swam over to the island and climbed up the tree on the outside, as the blacksnake always does, but when he put his head down into the hole the smoke choked him so that he fell into the burning stump, and before he could climb out again he was as black as the little racer.

Now they held another council, for still there was no fire, and the world was cold, but birds, snakes, and four-footed animals, all had some excuse for not going, because they were all afraid to venture near the burning sycamore, until at last the Water Spider said she would go. This was not the water spider that looked like a mosquito, but the other one, with black downy hair and red stripes on her body. She could run on top of the water or dive to the bottom, so there would be no trouble to get over to the island, but the question was, how could she bring back the fire? "I'll manage that, said the Water Spider; so she spun a thread from her body and wove it into a bowl, which she fastened on her back. Then she crossed over to the island and through the grass to where the fire was still burning. She put one little coal of fire into her bowl, and came back with it, and ever since we have had fire, and the Water Spider still keeps her bowl.

Source: Adapted from: "The First Fire," James Mooney, *Myths of the Cherokee. Nineteenth Annual Report of the Bureau of American Ethnology 1897–98, Part I.* (Washington, D.C.: U.S. Government Printing Office, 1900), pp. 241–242.

How the Child-of-the-Rain-God Rid the World of Monsters and Released the Birds of Summer

Traditionally, the Zuni of New Mexico were agriculturalists who depended on both irrigation and rainfall for their survival. Therefore, the prominent role of one of the Gods of Rain in the birth of a precocious hero is consistent with native beliefs linking rainfall to survival. In addition, Zuni theology asserted that harmony between humanity and the rest of the natural world is necessary for the maintenance of life. This philosophical theme is reinforced by the fact that Child-of-the-Rain-God's ability to accomplish miraculous feats arise from his kinship bonds to gopher, bat, and, of course, rain. The destruction of monsters and bestowal of gifts to humanity by a clever, but mischievous child (or often a pair of twins) is a common motif in Native American mythology.

In the days of the ancients, in a town under Thunder Mountain, there lived a most beautiful maiden. But one thing which struck the people who knew her was that she seldom came forth from her room, or went out of her house; never seemed to care for the people around her, never seemed to care to see the young men when they were dancing.

Now, this was the way of it. Through the roof of her room was a little skylight, open, and when it rained, one of the Gods of the Rain descended in the raindrops and wooed this maiden, and married her all unknown to her people; so that she was in his company every time it rained, and when the dew fell at night, on his ladder of water descending he came, and she was very happy, and cared not for the society of men. By and by, to the utter surprise of the people, whose eyes could not see this god, her husband, there was a little boy born to her.

He was the child of the gods, and, therefore, before he was many days old, he had begun to run about and speak, and had wonderful intelligence and wonderful strength and vivacity. He was only a month or two old when he was like a child of five, six, or eight years of age, and he would climb to the housetop and run down into the plaza and out around the village hunting birds or other small animals. With only his fingers and little stones for weapons, he never failed to slay and bring home these little creatures, and his mother's house was supplied more than any other house in the town with plumes for sacrifice, from the birds, which he captured in this way.

Finally, he observed that the older men of the tribe carried bows and arrows, and that the arrows went more swiftly and straighter than the stones he threw; and though he never failed to kill small animals, he found he could not kill the larger ones in that way. So he said to his mother one night: "Oh, mother, where does the wood grow that they make bows of, and where do they get sticks for their arrows? I wish you would tell me."

But the mother was quite silent; she did not like to tell him, for she thought it would lead him away from the town and something would happen to him. But he kept questioning her until at last she said, "Well, my little boy, if you go round the cliff here to the eastern side, there is a great hollow in the rocks, and down at the bottom of that hollow is a great cave. Now, around that shelter in the rocks are growing the trees out of which bows are made, and there also grow the bushes from which arrows are cut. They are so plentiful that they could supply the whole town, and furnish all the hunters here with bows and arrows, but they cannot get them, because in the cave lives a great bear, a very savage being, and no one dares go near there to get timber for the bows or sticks for the arrows, because the bear would surely devour whoever ventured there. He has devoured many of our people; therefore you must not go there to get these arrows. "No, indeed," said the boy. But at night he lay down with much in his mind, and was so thoughtful that he hardly slept the whole night. He was planning what he would do in the morning.

The next morning his mother was busy about her work, and finally she went down to the spring for some water, and the little boy slipped out of the house, ran down the ladder, went to the riverside, stooped down, and crawled along the bank of the river, until he could get around on the side of the cliff where the little valley of the spring that flows under Thunder Mountain lies. There he climbed up and up until he came to the shelter in the rocks round on the eastern side of Thunder Mountain. The mouth of this hollow was entirely closed with fine yellow-wood and oak, the best timber one would have for bows, and straight sprouts were growing everywhere out of which arrows could be made.

"Ah, this must be the place," said the boy, as he looked at it. I don't see any bear. I think I will climb up and see if there is anything to be afraid of, and try if I can cut a stick before the bear comes out."

He started and climbed into the mouth of the cavern, and his father, one of the Gods of the Rain, threw a tremendous shaft of lightning, and it thundered, and the cave closed together.

"Ha!" cried the boy. "What in the world is the meaning of this?" Then he stood there a moment, and presently the clouds finished and the cave opened, and all was quiet. He started to go in once more, and down came the lightning again, to remind him that he should not go in there.

"Ha!" cried the boy again. "What in the world does it mean?" And he rubbed his eyes, it had rather stunned him, and so soon as it had cleared away he tried again, and again for the fourth time.

Finally, the god said, "Ah! I have reminded him and he does not heed. He must go his own way." So the boy climbed into the cave.

No sooner had he got in than it began to get dark, and in came the bear on his hind legs and grabbed the boy and began to squeeze him very tight.

"O my! O my!" cried he. Don't squeeze me so hard! It hurts; don't squeeze me so hard! My mother is one of the most beautiful women you ever saw!"

"Hollo!" exclaimed the bear. "What is that you say?"

"My mother is one of the most beautiful women you ever saw!"

"Indeed!" said the bear, as he relaxed his hold.

"My son, sit down. What did you come to my house for? I am sure you are very welcome."

"Why," said the boy, "I came to get a piece of wood for a bow and sticks for arrows."

Said the bear, "I have looked out for this timber for a long time. There is none better in the whole country. Let me tell you what I will do. You don't look very strong. You haven't anything to cut the trees down with. I will go myself and cut down a tree for you. I will pick out a good one for a bow; not only that, but I will get fine sticks for arrows, too."

So he stalked off into the forest, and crack, crack, he smashed the trees down, and, picking out a good one, gnawed off the ends of it and brought it to the boy, then gathered a lot of fine straight sticks for arrow-shafts and brought them.

"There," said he, "take these home. Do you know how to make a bow, my son?"

"No, I don't very well," replied he.

"Well," said the Bear, "I have cut off the ends; make it about that length. Now take it home, and shave down the inside until it is thin enough to bend quickly at both ends, and lay it over the coals of fire so it will get hard and dry. That is the way to make a good bow."

"All right," said the boy; and as he took up the bundle of sticks and the stave for the bow, he said: "just come along toward night and I will introduce you to my mother."

"All right," said the old bear; "I will be along just about sunset. Then I can look at your bow and see whether you have made it well or not."

So the boy trudged home with his bundle of sticks and his bow stave, and when he arrived there his mother happened to be climbing out, and saw him coming.

"You wretched boy," she said, "I told you not to go out to the cave! I warrant you have been there where the bear stays!"

"Oh, yes, my mother; just see what I have brought," said the boy. "I sold you to the bear. He will be here to get you this evening. See what I have brought!" and he laid out his bow-timber and arrow-shafts.

"Oh," said she, "you are the most wretched and foolish of little boys; you pay no attention to what any one says to you; your mother's word is nothing but wind in your ears."

"Just see what I have brought home," said he. He worked as hard as he could to make his bow, stripped the arrow-shafts, smoothed and straightened them before the fire, and made the points of obsidian—very black it is; very hard and sharp were the points when he placed them on the arrows. Now, after placing the feathers on the arrows, he stood them up on the roof of the house against the parapet in the sunlight to dry; and he had his bow on the other side of the house against the other parapet to dry. He was still at work, toward sunset, when he happened to look up and saw the bear coming along, slowly, comfortably, rolling over the sand.

"Ah!" said he, "the old man is coming." He paid no attention to him, however.

Presently, the bear came close to the ladder, and shook it to see if it was strong enough to hold him.

"Are you coming?" asked the boy.

"Yes," said the Bear. "How have you been all day?"

"Happy," said the boy.

"How is your mother?"

"Happy," said the boy, "expecting you."

So the old bear climbed up. "Ah, indeed," said he, as he got over the edge of the house, "have you made the bow?"

"Yes, after a fashion."

So the bear went over, raised himself on his hind feet, looked at the bow, pulled it, and said, as he laid it down: "It is a splendid bow. What is this black stuff on these arrows?"

"Obsidian," answered the boy.

"These points are nothing but black coals," said the bear.

"I tell you," said the boy, "they are good, black, flint arrowheads, hard and sharp as any others."

"No," said the other, "nothing but coals."

"Now, suppose you let me try one of those coals on you," said the boy.

"All right," said the bear. He walked over to the other side of the roof and stood there, and the boy took one of the arrows, fitted it to the bow, and let go. It went straight into the heart of the bear, and even passed through him entirely.

"Wah!" uttered the Bear, as he gave a great snort and rolled over on the housetop and died.

"Ha, ha!" shouted the boy, "what you had intended to do unto me, thus unto you! Oh, mother!" called he, as he ran to the sky-hole, "here is your husband; come and see him. I have killed him; but, then, he would have me make the experiment," said the boy.

"Oh, you foolish, foolish, disobedient boy!" said the mother. What have you been doing now? Are we safe?

"Oh, yes," said he; "my stepfather is as passive as if he were asleep." And he went on and skinned his once prospective stepfather, and then took out his heart and hung it to the crosspiece of the ladder as a sign that the people could go and get all the bow-timber and arrows they pleased.

That night, after the evening meal was over, the boy sat down with his mother, and he said: "By the way, mother, are there any monsters or fearful creatures anywhere round about this country that kill people and make trouble?"

"No," said the mother, "none whatever."

"I don't know about that; I think there must be," said the boy.

"No, there are none whatever, I tell you," answered the mother.

The boy began to tumble on the floor, rolling about, playing with his mother's blankets, and throwing things around, and once in a while he would ask her again the same question, until finally she got very cross with him and said: "Yes, if you want to know, down there in the valley, beyond the great plains of sagebrush, is a den of Misho Lizards who are fearful and deadly to every one who goes near them. Therefore you had better be careful how you run round the valley."

"What makes them so fearful?" asked he.

"Well," said she, "they are venomous; they have a way of throwing from their mouths or breath a sort of fluid which, whenever it strikes a person, burns him, and whenever it strikes the eyes it blinds them. A great many people have perished there. Whenever a man arrives at their den they are very polite and greet him most courteously; they say: 'Come in; sit down right here in the middle of the floor before the fire.' But as soon as the person is seated in their house they gather round the walls and throw this venom on him, and he dies almost immediately."

"Is it possible?" responded the little boy; and for some reason or other he began to grow sleepy, and said: "Now, let us go to sleep, mother."

So he lay down and slept. Just as soon as it was light the next morning he aroused himself, dressed, took his bow and arrows, and, placing them in a corner near the ladder, said: "Oh, mother, give me my breakfast; I want to go and shoot some little birds. I would like to have some roasted birds for dinner."

She gave him his breakfast as quickly as she could, and he ran down the ladder and went to shooting at the birds, until he happened to see that his mother and others were out of sight; then he skulked into the sagebrush and went as straight as he could for the den of the Misho Lizards. There happened to be two young ones sunning themselves outside, and they said:

"Ah, my fine little fellow, glad to see you this morning. Come in, come in; the old ones will be very much pleased to entertain you. Come in!"

"Thank you," said the boy. He walked in, but he felt under his coat to see if a huge lump of rock salt he had was still there.

"Sit right down here," said the old people. The whole den was filled with these Misho Lizards, and they were excessively polite, every one of them.

The boy sat down, and the old Misho said to the young ones: "Hurry up, now; be quick!" And they began to throw their venom at him, and continued until he was all covered with it; but, knowing beforehand, and being the child of the gods, he was prepared and protected, and it did him no harm.

"Thank you, thank you," said the boy. "I will do the same thing. Then he pulled out the salt and pushed it down into the fire, where it exploded and entirely destroyed up the whole council of Misho Lizards.

"There!" cried the boy. "Thus would you have done unto me, thus unto you."

He took two fine ones and cut out their hearts, then started for home. When he arrived there, he climbed the ladder and suspended the two hearts beside that of the Bear and went down into the house, saying, "Well, mother, is dinner ready?"

"There now," said she, "I know it. I saw you hang those hearts up. You have been down there."

"Yes," said he, "they are all gone—every solitary one of them."

"Oh, you foolish, foolish, disobedient fellow! I am all alone in the world, and if you should go to some of those fearful places some time and not come back, who would hunt for me? What should I do?" said the mother.

"Don't be troubled, mother, now," said the boy. "I don't think I will go any more. There is nothing else of that kind around, is there, mother?"

"No, there is not," she replied; "not a thing. There may be somewhere in the world, but there is not anywhere here."

In the evening, as he sat with his mother, the boy kept questioning and teasing her to tell him of some other monsters—pulling on her skirts and repeating his questions.

"I tell you," she said, "there are no such creatures."

"Oh, mother, I know there are," said he, "and you must tell me about them."

So he continued to bother her until her patience gave out, and she told him of another monster. Said she, "If you follow that canyon down to the southeast, there is a very high cliff there, and the trail that goes over that cliff runs close by the side of a precipice. Now, that has been for ages a terrible place, for there is a Giant living there, who wears a hair-knot on his forehead. He lies there at length, sunning himself at his ease. He is very good-natured and very polite. His legs stretch across the trail on which men who pass that way have to go , and there is no other way to get by. And whenever a man tries to go by that trail, he says: 'Pass right along, pass right along;

I am glad to see you. Here is a fresh trail; some one has just passed. Don't disturb me; I am sunning myself.' Down below is the den where his children live, and on the flesh of these people he feeds them."

"Mercy!" exclaimed the boy. "Fearful! I never shall go there, surely. That is too terrible! Come, let us go to sleep; I don't want to hear anything more about it."

But the next morning, just as soon as daylight appeared, he got up, dressed himself, and snatched a morsel of food.

His mother said to him: "Where are you going? Are you thinking of that place I told you about?"

"No," said he; "I am going to kill some prairie-dogs right here in sight. I will take my war-club."

So he took his war-club, and thrust it into his belt in front, ran down the hill on which the village stood, and straightaway went off to the place his mother had told him of. When he reached the top of the rocks he looked down, and there, sure enough, laid the Giant with the forehead knot.

The Giant looked up and said: "Ah, my son, glad to see you this morning; glad to see you coming so early. Someone just passed here a little while ago; you can see his tracks there."

"Well," said the boy, "make room for me."

"Oh, just step right over," said the old man; "step right over me."

"I can't step over your great legs," said the boy; "draw them up."

"All right," said the old Demon. So he drew his knees up. "There, now, there is plenty of room; pass right along, my son."

Just as the boy got near the place, he thrust out his leg suddenly that way, to kick him off the cliff; but the boy was too nimble for him, and jumped aside.

"Oh, dear me," cried the Monster; "I had a stitch in my leg; I had to stretch it out."

"Ah," said the boy, "you tried to kick me off, did you?"

"Oh, no," said the old villain I had a terrible stitch in my knee," and he began to knead his knee in the most vehement manner. "Just pass right along; I trust it won't happen again."

The boy again attempted to pass, and the same thing happened as before.

"Oh, my knee! My knee!" exclaimed the Monster.

"Yes, your knee, your knee!" said the boy, as he whipped out his war-club and whacked the Giant on the head before he had time to recover himself. "Thus unto me you would have done, thus unto you!" said the boy.

No sooner had the Giant fallen than the little Top-knots gathered round him and began to eat; and they ate and ate and ate, (there were many of them) and they were voracious until they came to the top-knot on the old fellow's head, and then one of them cried; "Oh, dear, alas and alas! This is our own father!"

And while they were still crying, the boy cut out the Giant's heart and slung it over his shoulder; then he climbed down the cliff to where the young

Top-knots were, and slew them all except two,–a pair of them. Then he took these two, who were still young, like little children, and grasping one by the throat, wrung its neck and threw it into the air, when it suddenly became a winged creature, and spread out its wings and soared away, crying: "Peep, peep, peep," just as the falcons of today do. Then he took the other one by the neck, and swung it round and round, and flung it into the air, and it flew away with a heavy motion, and cried: "Boohoo, boohoo, boohoo!" and became an owl.

"Ah," said the boy, "born for evil, changed for good! Ye shall be the means whereby our children in the future shall sacrifice to the gods themselves."

Then he trudged along home with the Giant's heart, and when he got there, he hung it on the crosspiece of the ladder by the side of the other hearts. It was almost night then.

"There, now!" said his mother, as he entered the house; "I have been troubled almost to death by your not coming home sooner. You went off to the place I told you of; I know you did!"

"Ha!" said he, "of course I did. I went up there, and the poor fellows are all dead."

"Why will you not listen to me?" said she.

"Oh, it is all right, mother," said the boy. "It is all right." She went on scolding him in the usual fashion, but he paid no attention to her.

As soon as she had sat down to her evening tasks, he asked: "Now, is there any other of these terrible creatures?"

"Well, I shall tell you of nothing more now," said she.

"Why, is there anything more?" asked the boy.

"No, there is not," replied she.

"Ah, mother, I think there must be."

"No; there is nothing more, I tell you."

"Ah, mother, I think there must be."

And he kept bothering and teasing until she told him again, "Yes, away down in the valley, some distance from here, near the little Cold-making Hill, there lives a fearful creature, a gigantic Bison, more enormous than any other living thing. No one can go near him. He rushes stamping and bellowing about the country, and people never pass through that section from fear."

"Ah," said the boy don't tell me any more he must be a fearful creature, indeed."

"Yes; but you will be sure to go there," said she.

"Oh, no, no, mother; no, indeed!"

But the next morning he went earlier than ever, carrying with him his bows and arrows. He was so filled with dread, however, or pretended to be, that as he went along the trail he began to cry and sniffle, and walk very slowly, until he came near the hole of an old Gopher, his grandfather. The old fellow was working away, digging another cellar, throwing the dirt out, when he heard this crying. Said he: "That is my grandson; I wonder what he is up to now." So he ran and stuck his nose out of the hole he was digging, and said: "Oh, my grandchild, where are you doing?"

The boy stopped and began to look around.

"Right here! Right here!" cried the grandfather, calling his attention to the hole. "Come, my boy."

The boy put his foot in, and the hole enlarged, and he went down into it.

"Now, dry your eyes, my grandchild, and tell me what is the matter."

"Well," said the boy, "I was going to find the gigantic Bison. I wanted to take a look at him, but I am frightened!"

"Why, what is the matter? Why do you not go?" said the Gopher.

"Well, to tell you the truth, I thought I would try to kill him," he answered.

"Well, I will do what I can to help; you had better not try to do it alone. Sit here comfortably; dry your eyes, and I will see what I can do."

The old Gopher began to dig, dig, dig under the ground for a long way, making a fine tunnel, and packed it hard on the top and sides so that it would not fall in. He finally came to hear the "thud, thud, thud" of the heart of this creature, where it was lying, and dug the hole up to that spot. When he got there he saw the long layers of hair on its body, where no arrow could penetrate, and he cut the hair off, so that the skin showed white. Then he silently stole back to where the boy was and said: "Now, my boy, take your bow and arrows and go along through this hole until you get to where the tunnel turns upward, and then, if you look well, you will see a light patch. That is the skin next the heart of the gigantic Bison. He is sleeping there. You will hear the 'thud, thud, thud' of his heart. Shoot him exactly in the middle of that place, and then, mind you, turn around and run for your life, and the moment you get to my hole, tumble in, headforemost or any way."

So the boy did as he was told-crawled through the tunnel until he came to where it went upward, saw the light patch, and let fly an arrow with all his might, then rushed and scrambled back as hard as he could. With a roar that shook the earth the gigantic Bison fell over, then struggled to his feet, snorted, bellowed, and stuck his great horn into the tunnel, and like a flash of fire ripped it from end to end, just as the boy came tumbling into the deeper hole of his grandfather.

"Ah!" exclaimed the Gopher.

"He almost got me," said the boy.

"Sit still a moment and rest, my grandson," said the Gopher. "He didn't catch you. I will go and see whether he is dead."

So the Gopher stuck his nose out of the hole and saw there a great heap of flesh lying. He went out, nosed around, and smelt, jumped back, and went forward again until he came to the end of the creature, and then he took one of his nails and scratched out an eye, and there was no sign of life.

So he ran back to the boy, and said: "Yes, he breathes no more; you need not fear him longer."

"Oh, thank you, my grandfather!" said the boy. And he climbed out, and began to skin the beast. He took off its great thick skin, and cut off a suitable piece of it, for the whole pelt was so large and heavy that he could not carry it; then he took out the animal's great heart, and finally one of the large intestines and filled it with blood, then started for home. He went slowly, because his load was so heavy, and when he arrived he hung the heart on the ladder by the side of the others, and dragged the pelt to the sky-hole (hole in the ceiling of Zuni houses), and nearly scared the wits out of his mother by dropping it into the room.

"Oh, my child, now, here you are! Where have you been?" cried she. "I warned you of the place where the gigantic Bison was; I wonder that you ever came home."

"Ah, the poor creature," said the boy, "he is dead. Just look at this. He isn't handsome any more; he isn't strong and large any more."

"Oh, you wretched, wretched boy! You will be the death of me, as well as of yourself, some time," said the mother.

"No, mother," said the boy, "that is all nonsense."

That evening the boy said to his mother: "Now, mother, is there anything else of this kind left? If there is, I want to know it. Now, don't disappoint me by refusing to tell."

Oh, my dear son," said she, "I wish you wouldn't ask me; but indeed there is. There are terrible birds, great Eagles, fearful Eagles. In the very middle of an enormous cliff is a hollow place in the rocks where is built their nest, and there are their young ones. Day after day, far and near, they catch up children and young men and women, and carry them away, never more to be seen. These birds are more terrible than all the rest, because how can one get near to slay them? My son, I do hope and trust that you will not go this time, but, you foolish little boy, I see that you will go."

"Well, mother, let us go to sleep, and never mind anything about it," said the boy.

But after his mother had gone to sleep, he took the piece of rawhide he had skinned from the gigantic Bison, and, cutting it out, made himself a rawhide suit, skin-tight almost, so that it was perfectly smooth. Then he scraped the hair off, greased it all over, and put it away inside a blanket so that it would not dry. In the morning, quite early, he took his weapons, and taking also his rawhide suit, and the section of the gigantic Bison's intestine which he had filled with blood, he climbed the mesa near the Eagles' cliff. When he came within a short distance of the nest of the Eagles, he stopped and slipped on his rawhide suit, and tied the intestine of blood round his neck, like a sausage.

Then he began to cry and shake his head, and he cried louder than there was any need of his doing in reality; for presently the old father of the

Eagles, who was away up in the sky, just a mere speck, heard and saw him and came swishing down in a great circle, winding round and round the boy, and the boy looked up and began to cry louder still, as if frightened out of his wits, and finally rolled himself up like a porcupine, and threw himself down into the trail, crying and howling with apparent fear. The Eagle swooped down on him, and tried to grasp him in his talons, and his claws simply slipped off the rawhide coat. Then the Eagle made a fiercer grab at him and grew angry, but his claws would continually slip off, until he tore a rent in the intestine about the boy's neck, and the blood began to stream over the boy's coat, making it more slippery than ever. When the Eagle smelt the blood, he thought he had got him, and it made him fiercer than ever; and finally, during his struggling, he got one talon through a stitch in the coat, and he spread out his wings, and flew up, and circled round and round over the point where the young Eagles nest was, when he let go and shook the boy free, and the boy rolled over and over and came down into the nest; but he struck on a great heap of brush, which broke his fall. He lay there quite still, and the old Eagle swooped down and poised himself on a great crag of rock near by, which was his usual perching place.

"There, my children, my little ones," said he, "I have brought you food. Feast yourselves! Feast yourselves! For that reason I brought it."

So the little Eagles, who were very awkward, long-legged and short-winged, limped up to the boy and reached out their claws and opened their beaks, ready to strike him in the face. He lay there quite still until they got very near, and then said to them: "Shhsht!" And they tumbled back, being awkward little fellows, and stretched up their necks and looked at him, as Eagles will.

Then the old Eagle said: "Why don't you eat him? Feast yourselves, my children, feast yourselves!"

So they advanced again, more cautiously this time, and a little more determinedly too; and they reached out their beaks to tear him, and he said "Shhsht!" and, under his breath, "Don't eat me! And they jumped back again.

"What in the world is the matter with you little fools?" said the old Eagle. "Eat him! I can't stay here any longer; I have to go away and hunt to feed you; but you don't seem to appreciate my efforts much." And he lifted his wings, rose into the air, and sailed off to the northward direction.

Then the two young Eagles began to walk around the boy and examine him at all points. Finally, they approached his feet and hands.

"Be careful, be careful, don't eat me! Tell me about what time your mother comes home," said he, sitting up. "What time does she usually come?"

"Well," said the little Eagles, "she comes home when the clouds begin to gather and throw their shadow over our nest." (Really, it was the shadow of the mother Eagle herself that was thrown over the nest.)

"Very well," said the boy; "what time does your father come home?"

"When the fine rain begins to fall," said they, meaning the dew.

"Oh," said the boy. So he sat there, and by and by, sure enough, away off in the sky, carrying something dangling from her feet, came the old mother Eagle. She soared round and round until she was over the nest, when she dropped her burden, and over and over it fell and tumbled into the nest, a poor, dead, beautiful maiden. The young boy looked at her, and his heart grew very hot, and when the old Eagle came and perched, in a moment he let fly an arrow, and struck her down.

"Ha, ha!" exclaimed the boy. "What you have done to many, thus unto you."

Then he took his station again, and by and by the old father Eagle came, bearing a youth, fair to look upon, and dropped him into the nest. The young boy shut his teeth, and he said: "Thus unto many you have done, and thus unto me you would have done; so unto you." And he drew an arrow and shot him. Then he turned to the two young Eagles and killed them, and plucked out all the beautiful colored feathers about their necks, until he had a large bundle of fine plumes with which he thought to wing his arrows or to waft his prayers (by tying them to prayer sticks).

Then he looked down the cliff and saw there was no way to climb down, and there was no way to climb up. Then he began to cry, and sat on the edge of the cliff, and cried so loud that the old Bat Woman, who was gathering cactus berries below, or thought she was, overheard the boy.

Said she: "Now, just listen to that. I warrant it is my fool of a grandson, who is always trying to get himself into a scrape. I am sure it must be so." She spilled out all the berries she had found from the basket she had on her back, and then labored up to where she could look over the edge of the shelf.

"Yes, there you are," said she; "you simpleton! You wretched boy! What are you doing here?"

"Oh, my grandmother," said he, "I have got into a place and I cannot get out."

"Yes," said she; "if you were anything else but such a fool of a grandson and such a bard-hearted wretch of a boy, I would help you get down; but you never do as your mother and grandmother or grandfathers tell you."

"Ah, my grandmother, I will do just as you tell me this time," said the boy.

"Now, will you?" said she. "Now, can you be certain? Will you promise me that you will keep your eyes shut, and join me, at least in your heart, in the prayer which I sing when I fly down? Never open your eyes; if you do, the gods will teach you a lesson, and your poor old grandmother, too."

"I will do just as you tell me," said he, as he reached over and took up his plumes and held them ready.

"Not so fast, my child," said she; "you must promise me."

"Oh, my grandmother, I will do just as you tell me," said he.

"Well, step into my basket, very carefully now. As I go down I shall go very prayerfully, depending on the gods to carry so much more than I usually carry. Do you not wink once, my grandson."

"All right; I will keep my eyes shut this time," said he. So he sat down and squeezed his eyes together, and held his plumes tight, and then the old grandmother launched herself forth on her skin wings. After she had struggled a little, she began to sing.

" Now, just listen to that," said the boy; "my old grandmother is singing one of those tedious prayers; it will take us forever to go down."

Then, the old Bat Woman, perfectly unconscious of his state of mind, began to sing again.

"There she goes again," said he to himself, "I declare, I must look up; it will drive me wild to sit here all this time and hear my old grandmother try to sing."

Then, after a little while, she commenced singing again.

The boy stretched himself up, and said: "Look here, grandmother! I have heard your noise enough this time. I am going to open my eyes."

"Oh, my grandchild, never think of such a thing." Then she began to sing again. She was not near the ground when she finished it the fourth time, and the boy would not stand it any more. He opened his eyes, and the old grandmother knew it in a moment. Over and over, boy over bat, bat over boy, and the basket between them, they went whirling and pitching down, the old grandmother tugging at her basket and scolding the boy.

"Now, you foolish, disobedient one! I told you what would happen! You see what you have done!" and so on until they fell to the ground. It fairly knocked the breath out of the boy, and when he got tip again he yelled lustily.

The old grandmother picked herself up, stretched herself, and cried out anew: "You wretched, foolish, hard-hearted boy; I never will do anything for you again—never, never, never!"

"I know, my grandmother," said the boy, "but you kept up that noise so much. What in the world did you want to spend so much time chanting and buzzing round in that way for?"

"Ah, me!" said she, "he never did know anything—never will be taught to know anything."

"Now," said she to him, "you might as well come and eat with me. I have been gathering cactus-fruit, and you can eat and then go home." She took him to the place where she had poured out the contents of the basket, but there was scarcely a cactus berry. There were cedar berries, cones, sticks, little balls of dirt, coyote berries, and everything else inedible.

"Sit down, my grandson, and eat; strengthen yourself after your various adventures and exertions. I feel very weary myself," said she. And she took a nip of one of them; but the boy could not exactly bring himself to eat. The truth is, the old woman's eyes were bad, in the same way that bats' eyes are usually bad, and she could not tell a cactus berry from anything else round and rough.

"Well, inasmuch as you won't eat, my grandson," said she, "why, I can't conceive, for these are very good, it seems to me. You had better run along home now, or your mother will be killing herself thinking of you. Now, I have only one direction to give you. You don't deserve any, but I will give you one. See that you pay attention to it. If not, the worst is your own. You have gathered a beautiful store of feathers. Now, be very careful. Those creatures who bore those feathers have gained their lives from the lives of living beings, and therefore their feathers differ from other feathers. Heed what I say, my grandson. When you come to any place where flowers are blooming—where the sunflowers make the field yellow—walk round those flowers if you want to get home with these feathers. And when you come to more flowers, walk round them. If you do not do that, just as you came you will go back to your home."

"All right, my grandmother," said the boy. So, after bidding her goodbye, he trudged away with his bundle of feathers; and when he came to a great plain of sunflowers and other flowers he walked round them; and when he came to another large patch he walked round them, and then another, and so on; but finally he stopped, for it seemed to him that there were nothing but fields of flowers all the way home. He thought he had never seen so many before. "I declare," said he, "I will not walk round those flowers any more. I will hang on to these feathers, though."

So he took a good hold of them and walked in among the flowers. But no sooner had he entered the field than flutter, flutter, flutter, little wings began to fly out from the bundle of feathers, and the bundle began to grow smaller and smaller, until it wholly disappeared. These wings that flew out were the wings of the Sacred Birds of Summerland, made living by the lives that had supported the birds, which bore those feathers, and by coming into the environment, which they had so loved, the atmosphere that flowers always bring of summer.

Thus it was, my children, in the days of the ancients, and for that reason we have little jay-birds, little sparrows, little finches, little willow-birds, and all the beautiful little birds that bring the summer, and they always hover over flowers.

"My friends, that is the way we live. I am very glad, otherwise I would not have told the story, for it is not exactly right that I should—I am very glad to demonstrate to you that we also have books; only they are not books with marks in them, but words in our hearts, which have been placed there by our ancients long ago, even so long ago as when the world was new and young, like unripe fruit. And I like you to know these things, because people say that the Zuñis are people having no knowledge."

Thus shortens my story.

Source: Adapted from "How the Summer Birds Came," Frank Hamilton Cushing. *Zuni Folk Tales.* (New York: G.P. Putnam's Sons, 1901), pp. 65–92.

How Hunting and Farming Came to the Cherokee

The Cherokee of the Southeastern United States based their traditional lifestyle on farming and hunting supplemented by other occupations such as gathering wild plant foods. The following myth accounts for the origin of the two pillars of the Cherokee food supply and establishes a kinship between humans and both the plant and animal kingdoms. The motif of two brothers one of whom is "tame" while the other is "wild" and lives on the margins of society and the social order are distributed widely in Native American tradition.

When I was a boy, this is what the old men told me they had heard when they were boys.

Long ages ago, soon after the world was made, a hunter and his wife lived at Looking-glass Mountain, with their only child, a little boy. The father's name was Kanati, "The Lucky Hunter," and his wife was called Selu, "Corn." No matter when Kanati went into the woods, he never failed to bring back a load of game, which his wife cut up and prepared, washing the blood from the meat in the river near the house. The little boy used to play down by the river every day, and one morning the old people thought they heard laughing and talking in the bushes, as though there were two children there. When the boy came home at night, his parents asked who had been playing with him all day. "He comes out of the water," said the boy, and he calls himself my elder brother. He says his mother was cruel to him, and threw him into the river." Then they knew that the strange boy had sprung from the blood of the game which Selu had washed off at the river's edge.

Every day, when the little boy went out to play, the other would join him; but, as he always went back into the water, the old people never had a chance to see him. At last, one evening, Kanati said to his son, "Tomorrow, when the other boy comes to play with you, get him to wrestle with you, and when you have your arms around him hold on to him and call for us." The boy promised to do as he was told; so the next day, as soon as his playmate appeared, he challenged him to a wrestling-match. The other agreed at once, but as soon as they had their arms around each other Kanati's boy began to scream for his father. The old folks at once came running down, and when the wild boy saw them he struggled to free himself, and cried out, "Let me go! You threw me away!" But his brother held on until his parents reached the spot, when they seized the wild boy and took him home with them. They kept him in the house until they had tamed him, but he was always wild and artful in his disposition, and was the leader of his brother in every mischief. Before long the old people discovered that he was one of those persons endowed with magic powers, and they called him, "He who grew up Wild."

Whenever Kanati went into the mountains be always brought back a fat buck or doe, or may be a couple of turkeys. One day the wild boy said to his brother, "I wonder where our father gets all that game; let's follow him next time, and find out." A few days afterward, Kanati took a bow and some feathers in his hand, and started off. The boys waited a little while, and then started after him, keeping out of sight, until they saw their father go into a swamp where there were a great many of the reeds that hunters use to make arrow-shafts. Then the wild boy changed himself into a puff of bird's down, which the wind took up and carried until it alighted upon Kanati's shoulder just as he entered the swamp, but Kanati knew nothing about it. The hunter then cut reeds, fitted the feathers to them, and made some arrows, and the wild boy—in his other shape—thought, " I wonder what those things are for." When Kanati had his arrows finished, he came out of the swamp and went on again. The wind blew the down from his shoulder; it fell in the woods, when the wild boy took his right shape again, and went back and told his brother what he had seen. Keeping out of sight of their father, they followed him up the mountain until he stopped at a certain place and lifted up a large rock. At once a buck came running out, which Kanati shot, and then, lifting it upon his back, he started home again. "Oho!" said the boys, "he keeps all the deer shut up in that hole, and whenever he wants venison he just lets one out, and kills it with those things he made in the swamp." They hurried and reached home before their father, who had the heavy deer to carry, so that he did not know they had followed him.

A few days after, the boys went back to the swamp, cut some reeds and made seven arrows, and then started up the mountain to where their father kept the game. When they got to the place they lifted up the rock, and a deer came running out. Just as they drew back to shoot it, another came out, and then another, and another, until the boys got confused and forgot what they were about. In those days all the deer had their tails hanging down, like other animals, but, as a buck was running past, the wild boy struck its tail with his arrow so that it stood straight out behind. This pleased the boys, and when the next one ran by, the other brother struck his tail so that it pointed upward. The boys thought this was good sport, and when the next one ran past, the wild boy struck his tail so that it stood straight up, and his brother struck the next one so hard with his arrow that the deer's tail was curled over his back. The boys thought this was very pretty, and ever since the deer has carried his tail over his back.

The deer continued to pass until the last one had come out of the hole and escaped into the forest. Then followed droves of raccoons, rabbits, and all the other four-footed animals. Last came great flocks of turkeys, pigeons, and partridges that darkened the air like a cloud, and made such a noise with their wings that Kanati, sitting at home, heard the sound like distant thunder on the mountains, and said to himself, "My bad boys have got into trouble. I must go and see what they are doing."

So Kanati went up the mountain, and when he came to the place where he kept the game he found the two boys standing by the rock, and all the birds and animals were gone. He was furious, but, without saying a word, he went down into the cave and kicked the covers off four jars in one corner, when out swarmed bedbugs, fleas, lice, and gnats, and got all over the boys. They screamed with pain and terror, and tried to beat off the insects; but the thousands of insects crawled over them, and bit and stung them, until both dropped down nearly dead from exhaustion. Kanati stood looking on until he thought they had been punished enough, when be brushed off the vermin, and proceeded to give the boys a lecture. "Now, you rascals," said he, "you have always had plenty to eat, and never had to work for it. Whenever you were hungry, all I had to do was to come up here and get a deer or a turkey, and bring it home for your mother to cook. But now you have let out all the animals, and after this, when you want a deer to eat, you will have to hunt all over the woods for it, and then may be not find one. Go home now to your mother, while I see if I can find something to eat for supper."

When the boys reached home again they were very tired and hungry, and asked their mother for something to eat. "There is no meat," said Selu, "but wait a little while, and I will get you something." So she took a basket and started out to the provision-house—This provision-house was built upon poles high up from the ground, to keep it out of the reach of animals, and had a ladder to climb up by and one door, but no other opening. Every day, when Selu got ready to cook the dinner, she would go out to the provision-house with a basket, and bring it back full of corn and beans.

The boys had never been inside the provision-house, and wondered where all the corn and beans could come from, as the house was not a very large one; so, as soon as Selu went out of the door, the wild boy said to his brother, "Let's go and see what she does." They ran around and climbed up at the back of the provision-house, and pulled out a piece of clay from between the logs, so that they could look in. There they saw Selu standing in the middle of the room, with the basket in front of her on the floor. Leaning over the basket, she rubbed her stomach—so—and the basket was half-full of corn. Then she rubbed under her armpits—so—and the basket was full to the top with beans. The brothers looked at each other, and said, "This will never do; our mother is a witch. If we eat any of that it will poison us. We must kill her."

When the boys came back into the house, Selu knew their thoughts before they spoke? "So you are going to kill me! " said Selu.

"Yes," said the boys, "you are a witch."

"Well," said their mother, "when you have killed me, clear a large piece of ground in front of the house, and drag my body seven times around the circle. Then drag me seven times over the ground inside the circle, and stay up all night and watch, and in the morning you will have plenty of corn."

Then the boys killed her with their clubs, and cut off her head, and put it up on the roof of the house, and told it to look for her husband. Then they set to work to clear the ground in front of the house, but, instead of clearing the whole piece, they cleared only seven little spots. This is the reason why corn now grows only in a few places instead of over the whole world. Then they dragged the body of Selu around the circles, and wherever her blood fell on the ground the corn sprang up. But, instead of dragging her body seven times across the ground, they did this only twice, which is the reason why the Indians still work their crop but twice. The two brothers sat up and watched their corn all night, and in the morning it was fully grown and ripe.

When Kanati came home at last, he looked around, but could not see Selu anywhere, so he asked the boys where their mother was. "She was a witch, and we killed her," said the boys, "there is her head up there on top of the house."

When Kanati saw his wife's head on the roof he was very angry, and said, "I won't stay with you any longer. I am going to the Wolf people." So he started off, but, before he had gone far, the wild boy changed himself again to a tuft of down, which fell on Kanati's shoulder. When Kanati reached the settlement of the Wolf people, they were holding a council in the townhouse. He went in and sat down, with the tuft of bird's down on his shoulder. When the Wolf chief asked him his business, he said, "I have two bad boys at home, and I want you to go in seven days from now and play against them." Kanati spoke as though he wanted them to play a game of ball, but the wolves knew that he meant for them to come and kill the two boys. The wolves promised to go. Then the bird's down blew off from Kanati's shoulder, and the smoke carried it up through the hole in the roof of the townhouse. When it came down on the ground outside, the wild boy took his right shape again, and went home and told his brother all that he had heard in the townhouse. When Kanati left the Wolf people, he did not return home, but went on farther.

The boys then began to get ready for the wolves, and the wild boy—the magician—told his brother what to do. They ran around the house in a wide circle until they had made a trail all around it, excepting on the side from which the wolves would come, where they left a small open space. Then they made four large bundles of arrows, and placed them at four different points on the outside of the circle, after which they hid themselves in the woods and waited for the wolves. On the appointed day a whole army of wolves came and surrounded the house, to kill the boys. The wolves did not notice the trail around the house, because they came in where the boys had left the opening, but the moment they were inside the circle the trail changed to a high fence, and shut them in. Then the boys on the outside took their arrows and began shooting them down, and, as the wolves could not jump over the fence, they were all killed excepting a few, which escaped through the opening into a great swamp close by. Then the boys ran around the swamp, and a circle of fire sprang up in their tracks, and set fire to the grass and bushes, and burned up nearly all the other wolves. Only two or three got away, and these were all the wolves which were left in the whole world.

Soon afterward some strangers from a distance, who heard that the brothers had a wonderful grain from which they made bread, came to ask for some; for none but Selu and her family had ever known corn before. The boys gave them seven grains of corn, which they told them to plant the next night on their way home, sitting up all night to watch the corn, which would have seven ripe ears in the morning. These they were to plant the next night, and watch in the same way; and so on every night until they reached home, when they would have corn enough to supply the whole people. The strangers lived seven days' journey away. They took the seven grains of corn, and started home again. That night they planted the seven grains, and watched all through the darkness until morning, when they saw seven tall stalks, each stalk bearing a ripened ear. They gathered the ears with gladness, and went on their way. The next night they planted all their corn, and guarded it with wakeful care until daybreak, when they found an abundant increase. But the way was long and the sun was hot, and the people grew tired. On the last night before reaching home they fell asleep, and in the morning the corn they had planted had not even sprouted. They brought with them to their settlement what corn they had left, and planted it, and with care and attention were able to raise a crop. But ever since the corn must be watched and tended through half the year, which before would grow and ripen in a night.

As Kanati did not return, the boys at last concluded to go and see if they could find him. The wild boy got a wheel and rolled it toward the direction where it is always night. In a little while the wheel came rolling back, and the boys knew their father was not there. Then the wild boy rolled it to the south and to the north, and each time the wheel came back to him, and they knew their father was not there. Then he rolled it toward the Sun Land, and it did not return.

"Our father is there," said the wild boy, "let us go and find him." So the two brothers set off toward the east, and after traveling a long time they came upon Kanati, walking along, with a little dog by his side.

"You bad boys," said their father, "have you come here?"

"Yes," they answered; "we always accomplish what we start out to do. We are men!" "This dog overtook me four days ago," then said Kanati;

but the boys knew that the dog was the wheel which they had sent after him to find him. "Well," said Kanati, "as you have found me, we may as well travel together, but I will take the lead."

Soon they came to a swamp, and Kanati told them there was a dangerous thing there, and they must keep away from it. Then he went on ahead, but as soon as he was out of sight the wild boy said to his brother, "Come and let us see what is in the swamp." They went in together, and in the middle of the swamp they found a large panther, asleep. The wild boy got out an arrow, and shot the panther in the side of the head. The panther turned his head, and the other boy shot him on that side. He turned his head away again, and the two brothers shot together, but the panther was not hurt by the arrows, and paid no more attention to the boys.

They came out of the swamp, and soon overtook Kanati, waiting for them. "Did you find it?" asked Kanati.

"Yes," said the boys, "we found it, but it never hurt us. We are men." Kanati was surprised, but said nothing, and they went on again.

After a while Kanati turned to them, and said, "Now you must be careful. We are coming to a tribe called the Cookers. They are cannibals, and if they get you they will put you in a pot and feast on you." Then he went on ahead. Soon the boys came to a tree which had been struck by lightning, and the wild boy directed his brother to gather some of the splinters from the tree, and told him what to do with them.

In a little while they came to the settlement of the cannibals, who, as soon as they saw the boys, came running out, crying, "Good! Here are two nice, fat strangers. Now we'll have a grand feast!" They caught the boys and dragged them into the town ceremonial house, and sent word to all the people of the settlement to come to the feast. They made up a great fire, filled a large pot with water and set it to boiling, and then seized the wild boy and threw him into the pot, and put the lid on it. His brother was not frightened in the least, and made no attempt to escape, but quietly knelt down and began putting the splinters into the fire, as if to make it burn better. When the cannibals thought the meat was about ready, they lifted the lid from the pot, and that instant a blinding light filled the townhouse, and the lightning began to dart from one side to the other, beating down the cannibals until not one of them was left alive. Then the lightning went up through the smoke-hole, and the next moment there were the two boys standing outside the town ceremonial house as though nothing had happened.

They went on, and soon met Kanati, who seemed much surprised to see them, and said, "What! Are you here again?"

"Oh, yes, we never give up. We are great men!"

"What did the cannibals do to you?" "We met them, and they brought us to their townhouse, but they never hurt us." Kanati said nothing more, and they went on.

Kanati soon got out of sight of the boys, but they kept on until they came to the end of the world, where the sun comes out. The sky was just coming down when they got there, but they waited until it went up again, and then they went through and climbed up on the other side. There they found Kanati and Selu sitting together. The old folks received them kindly, and were glad to see them, and told them they might stay there a while, but then they must go to live where the sun goes down. The boys stayed with their parents seven days, and then went on toward the sunset land, where they are still living.

Source: Adapted from "Myths of the Cherokees," James Mooney. *Journal of American Folklore,* 1 (1888): 97–108, pp. 98–106.

The Origin and History of
the Jemez People

The Jemez have resided in New Mexico for 800 years. They share a dependence on agriculture as do the other Pueblos. The reliance on plant life is reflected in their origin myth by the emergence of humanity through the surface of the earth like a growing plant. Pest-ya-sode, according to some Jemez sources, is the Mexican monarch Montezuma reborn as a deity. The following narrative moves from the mythic period on to the legendary period of Navaho and Apache immigration into New Mexico. The tale concludes with the historical events surrounding the Pueblo Revolt of 1680, the reconquest of the Pueblos in 1694, and the Second Jemez Revolt and subjugation in 1696.

This earth is flat and round like a pancake and is known to possess four places of habitation, situated one above another. Each has for its roof the floor of the apartment above it, except this one, which has the sky. A long, long while ago our people lived in the apartment beneath this one. For a long time they lived there. Finally, one day a man saw a hole which led up through the roof to this world. He crawled up through it and all the people followed him.

The mouth of the hole opened into the cold of the far north. A council was called. At this meeting the elders decided to move toward the noonday sun. Said they, "The sun warmed the place from which we came; therefore, by moving towards it we will find a place where this earth becomes warmer."

So they began their march over mountains of ice and snow toward the boiling ocean. For a long, long time they journeyed, but the land of sunshine was not reached. On and on they marched till their food supply became scanty and their blankets became worn out. Then one by one the people began to die of cold and hunger. For a while those who survived kept up courage even under the adverse conditions, and continued their onward march. At last, however, their numbers being so depleted they became despondent and wished all to die.

Having pity on them, the mother god, the Moon, prayed to her husband, the Sun, to save the remnant of men, their children. So the Sun took one of the survivors of our people, painted his body in transverse black and white bands, decorated his hair with corn husks, and suspended eagle feathers behind each ear.

As soon as he was thus painted and decorated, this man became a *koshare* (a sacred clown) and began to dance, cut capers, and make grimaces. So interested did the people become in his performing that they forgot their sorrows and became glad. They then resumed their journey, which they continued till they reached the Rio Grande confluence.

Here in this valley they ceased their wanderings and took up their abode. Being few in numbers and not trained in the arts of war and defense, they were afraid of their savage neighbors who dwelt in the region. So they built their villages in narrow canyons, along cliffs, and in caves. In these they lived a great, great while, subsisting on the grain they raised and on the plentiful game.

Then the invading hordes began to make inroads into their territory. They killed all the game, or, by their presence, it was made unsafe to hunt. They took the fields one by one. They drove the people to the cliffs and caves; and then captured these strongholds by storm or starved the people until they came out of their own accord and gave themselves over to be slaughtered or to be enslaved. Only a few places still held out and these were reduced to such straits that their capture, followed by the massacre of the prisoners, was daily expected. Their annihilation was certain.

Again the mother god prayed to the Sun to save their children, and a second time the great father came to the rescue. This time, he placed among them a "knowing man," whose name was Pest-ya-sode.

Pest-ya-sode defeated the enemies, raised the siege of the cliffs and caves, and drove the savages out of the narrow canyons. He trained the people in the arts of war. He led them out into the open country. He at last expelled the hostile tribes from the region after a desperate encounter. He then instructed the Indians to build villages in horseshoe shape with continuous outer walls, so that they served both as places of residence and as fortifications. He taught them their religious rites and ceremonies. He instituted the sacred hunts. He taught the people to paint their houses and edifices of worship in representative figures of the gods. He made the clown dancers the sprouters of grain; the *koshare,* the maturers of grain and of everything that lives and grows upon the earth. To the god-clown dancers he gave power to represent men before the deities. To the medicine men he gave the power over "sickness" and over death. To the Sun priests and their aids he gave the power to intercede between those above and men.

For a long, long time he lived with them, extending their territory, building pueblos, and erecting edifices to the Sun. Finally, after he had made them a powerful and prosperous people, he called them all together and told them that there were many peoples that he must teach as he had taught them, and that he must go and instruct them. "Then," said he, "when I am gone you will neglect to do the things that I have taught you. Therefore will my father, the Sun, come in his wrath, destroy your pueblos, and give your fields to another race. After that will you return to do the things I have commanded you. Then when you have returned from your evil ways will I come on the wings of the morning, in the chariot of the Sun, expel the intruder from the land, restore your ancient possessions, and establish you in all your former glory."

After Pest-ya-sode had departed, the people did exactly what he said they would. They departed from keeping his sayings and commandments, and finally became divided. One division came to this valley; the remaining section staying at Pecos (New Mexico), the home of our tribe at the time Pest-ya-sode took his departure toward the boiling ocean. In this valley our people built village after village, only to have an earthquake throw them down or to have them razed to the ground by some of our many enemies. We have built villages on almost every square mile of land in this valley from the Rio Grande river to this place, a distance of a good day's walk; and, besides the ruins in the valley, thirteen of our deserted villages dot the mesa to the northward between here and the boiling springs. But yet we were still powerful. We still had seven villages in the valley of this river which bears our name. Here our people were admirably situated for farming. In the broad valley of the river and the valleys of its upper tributaries were large and good farms; while the great river always had water and to spare to irrigate the crops.

The scenery around the villages then was the same as that of the village now. To the north in Guadalupe canyon are the falls; and in the canyon of San Diego, the hot springs and soda dam. Still farther to the north are a forest-covered plateau and a great valley surrounded by obsidian cliffs and craters. To the northeast Mount Balda kisses the blue sky. To the east the Cochiti range shuts out the morning sun. To the southeast, across lava-capped mesas, our river joins the great river that flows in the direction of the sun at noon. Still farther southeast the high escarpment of the Sandia mountains rises abruptly from the plains. To the south are white-capped mesas; to the southwest, mesas and escarpments of stone so red that they reflect the rays of the morning sun, the reflected red light reaching even to this place. And to the west, the mountains, which have our name, give the sky a ragged horizon, while in the valleys are red and white domes and castled buttes.

With respect to defense, the situation of the villages then could scarcely have been bettered. The villages were walled. If defeated in the valley, our people could retreat to the isolated mesa at the forks of the river. There on its top they could make a decided stand against any enemy that might attack them, for its precipitous walls rise perpendicularly from the valley floor to eighty times the height of a man, and is only accessible by two narrow trails. But the evil day came when the Spanish arrived.

While under Spanish yoke the people built the village and church of San Juan de los Jemez at the boiling (Jemez) springs, and the village and church of San Jose de los Jemez, at Canyon, the ruins of both still remain. Then our people rose against this race of intruders and killed them all at the two villages. But more white people came and took possession of the land.

Against the place on the mesa both in 1694 and in 1696 they came with their cannon, and after a many days' battle each time they captured it, reducing it, finally, to the mass of ruins it is this day. Furthermore, at each of these times some of our people escaped to the Navajo country, but the greater part of them were captured and reduced to a state of servitude.

They then moved us all to the valley where we now live, and where we were joined by the remnant of the Pecos tribe in 1838. Since then, have we done penance and mortified our bodies to appease the wrath of our great father. And each morning at early dawn we send a man to the top of the mesa yonder to see if the great Pest-ya-sode is coming with his father on the wings of the morning to restore us our ancient possessions.

Source: Adapted from: "The Origin Story and the Mythical History of the Jemez People" Elsie Clews Parsons, *American Anthropologist,* 29 (1927): 722–726.

How the Snakes Acquired Their Poison

In their explanatory myth of the acquisition of poison by snakes, bees, and wasps, the Choctaw—who originally inhabited the Southeastern states of Mississippi, Alabama, and Louisiana—assess the personalities of snakes as well. The larger snakes, the rattler and the water moccasin, attack after warning or in self-defense. The smaller ground rattler, however, attacks from malice.

Long ago a certain vine grew along the edges of bayous, in shallow water. This vine was very poisonous, and often when the Choctaw would bathe or swim in the bayous they would come in contact with the vine and often become so badly poisoned that they would die as the result.

Now the vine was very kind and liked the Choctaw and consequently did not want to cause them so much trouble and pain. He would poison the people without being able to make known to them his presence there beneath the water. So he decided to rid himself of the poison. A few days later he called together the chiefs of the snakes, bees, wasps, and other similar creatures and told them of his desire to give them his poison, for up to that time no snake, bee or wasp had the power it now possesses, namely that of stinging a person.

The snakes and bees and wasps, after much talk, agreed to share the poison.

The rattlesnake was the first to speak and he said: "I shall take the poison, but before I strike or poison a person I shall warn him by the noise of my tail; then if he does not heed me I shall strike."

The water moccasin was the next to speak, "I also am willing to take some of your poison; but I shall never poison a person unless he steps on me."

The small ground rattler was the last of the snakes to speak, "Yes I will gladly take of your poison, and I will also jump at a person whenever I have a chance."

And so it has continued to do ever since.

Source: Adapted from "Myths of the Louisiana Choctaw," David I. Bushnell, Jr. *American Anthropologist* 12 (1910): pp. 526–535, p. 533.

HEROES, HEROINES,
VILLAINS, AND FOOLS

Destroyer-of-Dangerous-Things: An Apache Hercules

The following myth of the Jicarilla Apache of New Mexico passes quickly from the emergence and development of life on the surface of the present world to the adventures of Destroyer-of-Dangerous-Things. Like the demigod Hercules (Greek, Heracles), the Jicarilla monster slayer cleansed the environment, making it safe for human habitation. The influence of their Native American neighbors the Taos Pueblos is evident in both the frequent references made to the latter and in the emergence of the first humans from an unpleasant subterranean world, a motif that is likely to have been borrowed from the Pueblos by the nomadic Apache after their migration into the southwestern states in the early 16th century.

In the beginning the earth was covered with water, and all living things were below in the underworld. Then people could talk, the animals could talk, the trees could talk, and the rocks could talk.

It was dark in the underworld, and they used eagle plumes for torches. The people and the animals that go about by day wanted more light, but the night animals—the bear, the panther, and the owl—wanted darkness. They disputed long, and at last agreed to play the hidden button game to decide the matter. It was agreed that if the day animals won there should be light, but if the night animals won it should be always dark.

The game began, but the magpie and the quail, which love the light and have sharp eyes, watched until they could see the button through the thin wood of the hollow stick, and they told the people under which one it was. They played once, and the people won. The morning star came out and the black bear ran and hid in the darkness. They played again, and the people won. It grew bright in the east and the brown-bear ran and hid himself in a dark place. They played a third time, and the people won. It grew brighter in the east and the mountain-lion slunk away into the darkness. They played a fourth time, and again the people won. The Sun came up in the east, and it was day, and the owl flew away and hid himself.

Still the people were below and did not see many things, but the Sun staid higher up and saw more. The Sun looked through a hole and saw that there was another world, this earth above. He told the people and they wanted to go there; so they built four mounds by which to reach the upper world. In the east they built a mound and planted it with all kinds of fruits and berries that were black in color. In the south they built another mound and planted on it all kinds of fruits that were blue. In the west they built another mound and planted upon it fruits that were yellow; and in the north they built a mound, and on it they planted all fruits of variegated colors.

The mounds grew into mountains and the bushes went from blossom to ripened berries, and one day two girls climbed up to pick berries and to gather flowers to tie in their hair. Then the mountains stopped growing because of the girls' interference. The people wondered, and they sent Tornado to learn the cause. Tornado goes everywhere and searches into every corner, and he found the two girls picking berries on the mountain, and he came back and told the people. Then they sent Tornado again to bring the girls home, and he brought them back to their people, but the mountains did not grow any more.

The mountains had stopped growing while their tops were yet a long way from the upper world, and the people debated how they could get up to the earth. They laid feathers crosswise for a ladder, but the feathers were too weak and they broke. They made a second ladder of larger feathers, but again they were too weak. They made a third ladder, of eagle feathers, but even these were not strong enough to bear their weight. Then the buffalo came and offered his right horn to make a ladder, and three others came and offered their right horns also. The buffalo horns were strong, and by their help the people were able to climb up through the hole to the surface of the earth; but their weight bent the buffalo horns, which before were straight, so that they have been curved ever since.

When the people had come up from under the earth, they fastened the sun and moon with spider threads, so that they could not get away, and sent them up into the sky to give light. But water covered the whole earth, so four storms went to roll the waters away. Black-storm blew to the east and rolled up the waters into the eastern ocean. Blue-storm blew to the south and rolled up the waters in that direction. Yellow-storm rolled up the waters in the west, and the Varicolored-storm went to the north and rolled up the waters there. So were formed the four oceans in the east, the south, the west, and the north. Having rolled up the waters, the Storms returned to where the people were waiting at the mouth of the hole.

First went out the skunk, but the ground was still soft, and his legs sank in the black mud and remain black ever since. They sent Tornado to bring him back, for the time was not yet. The badger went out, but he, too, sank in the mud, and his legs were blackened, so they sent Tornado to call him back. The beaver went out, wading through the mud and swimming through the water. He began at once to build a dam to save the water still remaining in pools, and he did not return. Tornado was sent after him and found him at work, and asked him why he had not come back.

"Because I wanted to save the water for the people to drink," said the beaver.

"Good," said Tornado, and they went back together. They waited again, and then sent out the Crow to see if it was yet time. The Crow found the earth dry, and many dead frogs, fish, and reptiles lying on the ground. He began picking out their eyes, and did not return until Tornado was sent after him. The people were angry when they found he had been eating carrion, and they changed his color to black, which before was gray.

The earth was now all dry, excepting the four oceans around it and the lake in the center, where the beaver had dammed up the waters. All the people came up. They went east until they came to the ocean; then they turned south until they came again to the ocean; then they turned west until they came again to the ocean, and then they turned north, and as they went each tribe stopped where it would. But the Jicarillas continued to circle around the place where they had come up from the underworld. Three times they went around, when the Creator became displeased, and asked them where they wished to stop.

They said, "In the middle of the earth." So he led them to a place very near to Taos (New Mexico) and left them there, and the Taos Indians lived near them.

Then he laid down the great mountains. He made also the four great rivers and gave them their names in the north the Napeshtl, the "flint arrow" river (the Arkansas River); in the east the Canadian; in the south the Rio Grande, and in the west the Chama, and he gave the country to the Jicarillas. He made other rivers, but did not give them names.

While the Jicarillas were moving about they by accident left a girl behind them near the place where they had come up from the underworld. The girl's name was the "White-bead woman." The sun shone upon her as she sat and she bore a boy child, and the moon beamed upon her as she slept and bore another boy child. The first born was stronger than the second, as the sun is stronger than the moon. When the boys were large enough to walk the Sun told her where to find her people, and she went to them.

The boys lived with their mother near Taos. She made them a wheel-and-stick game to play with, and told them not to use the stick to roll the wheel toward the north. They played three days, and the Sun's son rolled the wheel toward the east, the south, and the west, when his brother persuaded him to roll it toward the north to see what would happen. Then he rolled the wheel toward the north, and it rolled without stopping until it was out of sight. The boys decided to go after it, and they followed its track along the ground until they came to a house built like a Pueblo house.

The wheel had gone around to the north side and was lying upon the flat roof. Owl lived in the house. He heard a noise outside, and sent his child to see what was there. The young owl climbed up the ladder and looked out the doorway on the roof and saw the wheel lying there and the boys standing below. He got the wheel and then called the boys, but they would not come. Then old Owl went and called the boys, and they came into the house. They asked for their wheel, which they saw hanging up on the wall, but old Owl called his wife and told her to build a fire and fill the pot with water. When the water was boiling he seized the boys and put them into the pot. When he thought the meat was cooked he took the pot from the fire and dipped the boys out with a large spoon, but they were both alive and asked for their wheel.

He put them under the ashes to bake, but when he took them out they were alive and asked again for their wheel. Owl said no more, but gave them their wheel, and they returned home to their mother.

Soon afterward Sun sent word to the woman to send his son to him. The Moon-boy stayed at home with his mother, but the Sun-boy went and found his father at home. His father received him kindly and gave him a bow and arrows and a tunic of turquoise, with turquoise bracelets and wrist-guard and a necklace of turquoise beads for his neck. Then Sun said to him, "Now you shall be called the Destroyer-of-dangerous-things because I shall send you to destroy many dangerous things which annoy the people."

His father told him to go first against a great Frog, which lived under tile water in a lake by Taos and sucked in everybody who came near. His breath was like sheet lightning at night, and he had sucked so many people under the water that there were very few Taos Indians remaining.

The boy left his turquoise dress and weapons with his father and went as a poor boy, with torn clothing and neglected hair. He came to Taos and asked the people for food, but they laughed at his appearance and refused him food or shelter. He went away and slept outside the pueblo. It was winter, but he was the son of the Sun and the cold could not hurt him. The Pueblo storerooms were full of corn. The boy outside waved his hand, and all the grains disappeared from the cobs, and instead were only white worms. In the morning, when the Pueblos found the corn all gone, they were sorry for the way they had treated the boy, who they now knew was a wonder-worker, so they went to him and asked his pardon. The boy forgave them and waved his hand, and again the white grains of corn were on the cob.

Now they gave him plenty of corn and bread, and he had a good dinner. Then they told him about the great Frog and asked his help in the matter. He promised to help them, and after he had eaten he went out and went up, like a lightning flash, to his father, the Sun, to get his turquoise dress and his weapons. His father gave him also a wheel of black stone, a wooden wheel of blue, another wheel of yellow stone, and a varicolored wheel of wood. He gave him likewise four fire-sticks, black, blue, yellow, and varicolored.

When the boy returned to Taos and the Pueblos saw how finely he was dressed, they gave him a large armlet of red coral beads for his right arm and another of white shell beads for his left arm. He went down to the lake and stood on the east shore early in the morning as the Sun was coming up. The Frog put his head up from the lake and tried to suck him in, but the boy could not be moved, and the Frog dived under the water again. Then the boy threw the wheel of black stone into the center of the lake, and the water fell a little. He went around to the south shore and threw in the blue wheel, and the water fell yet a little more. He stood on the west shore and threw in the yellow wheel, and the water grew shallow and muddy. Then he went around to the north and threw in the varicolored wheel of wood, and at once the water was dried up, and he saw the Frog's house in the center of the lake, like a Pueblo house, with four doors, one on each side, and a row of stepping stones from each door to the edge of the lake.

He went around to the east side of the lake, where he had stood at sunrise, and crossed over on the stepping stones to the first door. On each side of the door stood guard a Pueblo Indian who had been sucked in by the Frog. They had been put there to warn the Frog should an enemy approach; but the boy only spoke to them, and they were unable to move. At the south door he found two bears on guard, sitting upon their haunches. At the west door he found two immense snakes, with heads erect and hissing, and at the north door he found two panthers. To each in turn he spoke, and they were motionless and allowed him to pass. Then he went inside the house, and there he found the Great Frog sitting in a room from which a door opened on each of the four sides.

He asked the Frog where were all the people who had been sucked into the lake, but the Frog said he knew nothing about them. The boy knew this was not true, so he took out his four fire-sticks and twirled them rapidly until the room was full of thick smoke that choked the Frog, and it fell down dead. Then he told the two Pueblo guards to release their people, and they opened the four doors around the sides of the room, and all the rooms were filled with Pueblos who had been sucked under the water by the Frog. There were also a great many little frogs, the children of the Great Frog; but they were too small to be dangerous, so the boy let them live, but told them they should never grow larger. From them came the present small frogs. The boy returned to Taos with all the people he had set free from under the water. The Pueblos were very grateful to have their friends restored to them and invited him to bring his mother and brother to Taos for anything they needed. He brought them there to visit for a while, and then went back to his father, the Sun, to see what was for him to do next. His mother and brother were afraid to stay alone, on account of the many dangerous things in the world, so they did not go back to their own camp, but remained with their friends at Taos.

When Destroyer-of-dangerous-things came again, like a lightning flash, to his father, the Sun told him he must now go and destroy a dangerous Elk, who lived near a lake and ranged over the whole Jicarilla country. This Elk was of immense size—his youngest child was larger than any elk we know now—and very fierce and swift, so that he could overtake any one whom he pursued, and always tore him to pieces with his horns.

His father gave him four flat round stones and four fire-sticks—black, blue, yellow, and particolored—together with a bolt of lightning, and the boy took them and started to look for the Elk. He went first to the lake, but the Elk was not there, and he continued the search until at last he found the Elk upon a mountain, lying down with his face toward the east, on the lookout for any traveler who might be coming across the plain.

While the boy was wondering how he could approach the Elk without being seen, Gopher came up, to whom he told his story. Gopher agreed to help him, and made a long circuit around to the east of the mountain, where he went under the ground and dug a tunnel all the way until he came up under the left shoulder of the Elk, where he was lying down. He dug right up to the Elk's heart. The Elk felt the earth move, and looking around he saw the Gopher and asked him what he wanted.

Gopher said his little ones were cold, and he only wanted a little hair to line their nest. The Elk said that was all right, so the Gopher pulled out a tuft of hair from directly over the Elk's heart. He dug a deep hole below the Elk, and then came back and told the boy. Destroyer, with his bow and arrows, fire-sticks, the flat stones, and the lightning bolt, entered the tunnel and went on until he came up under the Elk and could feel the throbbing of his heart where the Gopher had pulled out the hair. He fitted an arrow to his bow and shot the Elk through from one shoulder to the other. The Elk jumped to his feet and looked all around for the enemy.

With the bolt of lightning from his father the boy shot his first fire-stick to the east, where it made a black smoke. The Elk ran in that direction, but found no one there. In the same way the boy shot the second fire-stick to the south, where it raised a blue smoke. The Elk went toward it, but slowly now, for his wound was taking his strength, and found nothing there. With the lightning bolt the boy shot the third fire-stick to the west, and it made a yellow smoke. The Elk went toward it, slowly now, for he was dying, but found nothing. Then the boy shot his last fire-stick to the north, and it raised a smoke of various colors.

The Elk went after it, but found nothing, and came back with his lifeblood gushing from his mouth, to die where he had first lain down. In the meantime the boy had made preparation by piling the four flat rocks, one above another, over the hole in which he was hiding. The Elk saw them and knew his enemy must be there. With a last effort he lowered his horns and charged upon them. He charged once, and the black rock was split in pieces; twice, and the blue rock under it was shivered; again, and the yellow rock was broken. Only the particolored rock now remained to protect the boy, but as the Elk lowered his horns again he rolled over dead and the whole earth trembled.

The great dangerous Elk had smaller children. The boy did not kill these, but told them they must never grow larger, and from them have come the Elk that we know. He gave a part of the meat to the Gopher and brought the rest to his mother and brother and their friends at Taos. On command of his father, the Sun, he dried the skin of the Elk and made of it a coat with the hair inside and large enough to cover his whole body, all but his eyes, and laced it along the front. The blood, he saved in an entrail and tucked it inside his coat, together with the two antlers of the Elk, one black and one red. Then he returned to his father to learn what more there was for him to do.

His father told him he must go next to destroy two great eagles that lived on "Standing-rock," a high, steep cliff westward from Taos, with two sharp peaks on the eastern and the western ends and a depression in the center between them. They had two young ones in the nest. From their perch upon the two high peaks they kept watch over all the country below, and whenever either saw an Indian traveling alone he would swoop down upon him, bear him up in his talons high above the cliff, and dash the life out of him on the rocks below, that the young eagles might have food.

Taking his coat of elk skin with the entrails full of blood and the two horns, as directed by his father, the boy traveled on to Standing Rock and stopped at the base of the eagle cliff. There he put on his elk-skin coat, with the hair inside, put the entrails and the two horns in front of his coat and laced it all tightly across in front. Then he lay down and waited. Soon the male eagle saw him and swooped down and tried to strike his talons into the boy's body. Three times he struck at him as the boy lay flat upon the ground, but the sharp claws only slipped off from the smooth elk skin. Then the boy turned over and the eagle fastened his claws into the lacing of the coat and carried the boy high up above the cliff and dashed him down near the nest. The blood from the entrails was spilled upon the rock, and the eagle thought the boy was dead and told the young birds to go and eat.

As the young eagles came near to tear him in pieces the boy made a hissing sound, "S-s!" and they were frightened and ran back to their father. "What kind of meat have you brought us? It whistles and we don't think it is dead."

Their father said, "It is the wind that whistles through the hole where my claws struck. Go back and eat." Then the old eagle flew away and left the young ones alone with the boy.

The young eagles came near again and the boy caught them and held them fast. "When does your father come back and where does he sit?"

The young birds answered, "When it hails he will come and he sit on the east peak."

"And when does your mother come and where does she sit?"

They answered, "When it rains she will come and will sit on the western peak."

The Destroyer went and hid himself behind a shelf of the eastern peak. Very soon it began to hail and he got out his black elk horn and watched.

Then he heard a man cry, and looking up he saw the male eagle coming with a Pueblo Indian in his talons. The old eagle came near and dashed the man down upon the rock and killed him, and then settled down upon the high peak to rest and flap his wings. The boy crept out from behind the rock and threw the elk horn so that it struck the eagle in the back of the head and killed him, and the eagle tumbled off the peak and fell clear down to the bottom of the cliff.

The boy went and hid behind the western peak. Soon it began to rain, and he saw the mother eagle coming with another Indian in her claws. She threw the man down upon the rock and killed him, and then flew up upon the peak to rest. The boy struck her with his red elk horn, and she fell dead to the bottom of the cliff. Then he came out from behind the rock and went over to the two young eagles in the nest. He did not kill them, but told them they must never grow any larger, and eagles have remained of that size ever since.

Now, the boy wanted to go back to his father, but the cliff was very steep and high and there was no way to climb down to the bottom. He walked round and round on the top of the rock, but found no way to get down. Toward evening, when it was getting dark, he saw Bat flying below near the base of the rock, and Bat had a basket. The boy called to him once and again, and at last Bat heard and asked him what he wanted. The boy said, "If you will take me down from this rock, I will give you some eagle feathers." Everybody knows what eagle feathers are worth, so Bat said he would do it, and he circled round and round the rock, because it was too steep to fly directly up, until he reached the top.

He had the basket tied to his body with spider threads, and at first the boy was afraid to get in, but Bat encouraged him and told him to get in and keep his eyes shut and he would be all right, but if he forgot and opened his eyes he would get dizzy and would fall out and be killed; so the boy got into the basket, and Bat began to go down by circling around the rock in the same way that he had come. He went very slowly, and once the boy got tired and wanted to open his eyes; but Bat knew his thoughts and warned him again, and the boy kept his eyes shut, and at last they were down.

The Destroyer went over to the dead eagles and pulled out the small white feathers from their breasts and wings and filled Bat's basket with them. He stretched out the male eagle to face the east and its mate to face the west, and then brought the basket of feathers and gave them to Bat.

The boy went to Taos to see his mother and brother, and then returned to see what more his father, the Sun, had for him to do. His father told him of still other dangerous things which must be exterminated before the people could go about their affairs in safety.

He was sent next by his father to destroy two giant Bears that lived in a mountain west from Santa Clara and ravaged the whole country around. The Indian arrows only glanced from the bodies of the animals without harming them, but the boy's father showed him how to kill the he-bear by shooting him through the heart, which was in the palm of his right fore foot. The she-bear was killed by a bolt of lightning darted by the Sun himself. The bodies were burnt and the two cubs were commanded to grow no larger, and bears remain of that size ever since.

There was also a rock, known as "Rock-that-runs," which lived at Cieneguilla, east of the Rio Grande and southwest of Taos. The rock was alive and had a head and a mouth and used to roll after people and overtake and crush them and then swallow them. By the help of his father, the Sun, the boy shot an arrow through the rock and killed it. The rock is still tilere, lying on a level flat-a black rock as large as a house, with its "face " to the west, and with a spot on the north and on the south side where the arrow went through, and red streaks running down from them were the blood ran down to the ground.

Other monsters he destroyed, until at last his father told him there was only one more left. This was a great winged fish which dwelt in a lake somewhere in the west and lived upon human hearts. It used to fly above the trails and dart down upon its victims, crushing in their breastbone to get at the heart. The Sun gave this last work to the Moon-boy, who had stayed at home all this time to take care of his mother. The two brothers went on together until they came to the lake and waited for the great fish to fly out. When it came the Moon-boy struck it on the head and stunned it with a lightning bolt, which the Sun had given him. Then as it lay motionless he shot four arrows into its heart. Cutting the body open, he lifted out the heart upon the four arrows and thrust it into the moon, and we see it there now.

When their work was done and the world was made safe, the boys said their last words to the people and started after the Sun along the trail to the west. Twelve men went with them. As they journeyed they came to twelve mountains, one after another, and inside of each mountain the brothers placed a man to wait forever until their return. They went on and on until they went into the western ocean, where they are living now in a house of turquoise under the green water.

Source: Adapted from "The Jicarilla Genesis," James Mooney. *American Anthropologist,* 11(1898): 197–209.

Blood Clot Boy

Among the Blackfoot, a nomadic Plains culture who relied on buffalo hunting, polygyny was an option, especially for more affluent men. Marriage to sisters, as portrayed in the following narrative, was the form this marriage custom usually took. The behavior of Blood Clot Boy's brother-in-law, however, violates the primary social norms of the group thus setting the tale in motion. The hero's exploits reinforce traditional Blackfoot values: hospitality, sharing, cooperation, and respect for elders. Each of his adversaries has violated these principles in one way or another and receives immediate justice from Blood Clot Boy.

Once there was an old man and woman whose three daughters married a young man. The old people lived in a lodge by themselves. The young man was supposed to hunt buffalo, and feed them all. Early in the morning the young man invited his father-in-law to go out with him to kill buffalo. The old man was then directed to drive the buffalo through a gap where the young man stationed himself to kill them as they went by. As soon as the buffalo were killed, the young man requested his father-in-law to go home. He said, "You are old. You need not stay here. Your daughters can bring you some meat." Now the young man lied to his father-in-law; for when the meat was brought to his lodge, he ordered his wives not to give meat to the old folks. Yet one of the daughters took pity on her parents and stole meat for them. The way in which she did this was to take a piece of meat in her robe, and as she went for water drop it in front of her father's lodge.

Now every morning the young man invited his father-in-law to hunt buffalo; and, as before, sent him away and refused to permit his daughters to furnish meat for the old people. On the fourth day, as the old man was returning, he saw a clot of blood in the trail, and said to himself, "Here at least is something from which we can make soup." In order that he might not be seen by his son-in-law, he stumbled, and spilt the arrows out of his quiver. Now, as he picked up the arrows, he put the clot of blood into the quiver. Just then the young man came up and demanded to know what it was he picked up. The old man explained that he had just stumbled, and was picking up his arrows. So the old man took the clot of blood home and requested his wife to make blood-soup. When the pot began to boil, the old woman heard a child crying. She looked all around, but saw nothing. Then she heard it again. This time it seemed to be in the pot. She looked in quickly, and saw a boy baby, so she lifted the pot from the fire, took the baby out and wrapped it up.

Now the young man, sitting in his lodge, heard a baby crying, and said, "Well, the old woman must have a baby." Then he sent his oldest wife over to see the old woman's baby, saying, "If it is a boy, I will kill it." The woman came in to look at the baby, but the old woman told her it was a girl. When the young man heard this, he did not believe it. So he sent each wife in turn; but they all came back with the same report.

Now the young man was greatly pleased, because he could look forward to another wife. So he sent over some old bones, that soup might be made for the baby. Now, all this happened in the morning.

That night the baby spoke to the old man, saying, "You take me up and hold me against each lodge-pole in succession." So the old man took up the baby, and, beginning at the door, went around in the direction of the sun, and each time that he touched a pole the baby became larger. When halfway around, the baby was so heavy that the old man could hold him no longer. So he put the baby down in the middle of the lodge, and, taking hold of his head, moved it toward each of the poles in succession, and, when the last pole was reached, the baby had become a very fine young man. Then this young man went out, got some black flint [obsidian] and, when he got to the lodge, he said to the old man, "I am the Smoking-Star. I came down to help you. When I have done this, I shall return."

Now, when morning came, Blood-Clot (the name his father gave him) arose and took his father out to hunt. They had not gone very far when they killed a scabby cow. Then Blood-Clot lay down behind the cow and requested his father to wait until the son-in-law came to join him. He also requested that he stand his ground and talk back to the son-in-law. Now, at the usual time in the morning, the son-in-law called at the lodge of the old man, but was told that he had gone out to hunt. This made him very angry, and he struck at the old woman, saying, "I have a notion to kill you." So the son-in-law went out.

Now Blood-Clot had directed his father to be eating a kidney when the son-in-law approached. When the son-in-law came up and saw all this, he was very angry. He said to the old man, "Now you shall die for all this."

"Well," said the old man, "you must die too, for all that you have done." Then the son in-law began to shoot arrows at the old man, and the latter becoming frightened called on Blood-Clot for help. Then Blood-Clot sprang up and upbraided the son-in-law for his cruelty.

"Oh," said the son-in-law, "I was just fooling." At this Blood-Clot shot the son-in-law through and through.

Then Blood-Clot said to his father, "We will leave this meat here: it is not good. Your son-in-law's house is full of dried meat. Which one of your daughters helped you?" The old man told him that it was the youngest. Then Blood-Clot went to the lodge, killed the two older women, brought up the body of the son-in-law, and burned them together. Then he requested the younger daughter to take care of her old parents, to be kind to them. "Now," said Blood-Clot, "I shall go to visit the other people."

So he started out, and finally came to a camp. He went into the lodge of some old women, who were very much surprised to see such a fine young man. They said, "Why do you come here among such old women as we? Why don't you go where there are young people?"

"Well," said Blood-Clot, "give me some dried meat." Then the old women gave him some meat, but no fat. "Well," said Blood-Clot, "you did not give me the fat to eat with my dried meat."

"Hush!" said the old women. "You must not speak so loud. There are bears here that take all the fat and give us the lean, and they will kill you, if they hear you."

"Well," said Blood-Clot, "I will go out tomorrow, do some butchering, and get some fat." Then he went out through the camp, telling all the people to make ready in the morning, for he intended to drive the buffalo over the cliff .

Now there were some bears who ruled over this camp. They lived in a bear-lodge and were very cruel. When Blood-Clot had driven the buffalo over, he noticed among them a scabby cow. He said, "I shall save this for the old women."

Then the people laughed, and said, "Do you mean to save that poor old beast? It is too poor to have fat." However, when it was cut open it was found to be very fat. Now, when the bears heard the buffalo go over the drive, they as usual sent out two bears to cut off the best meat, especially all the fat; but Blood-Clot had already butchered the buffalo, putting the fat upon sticks. He hid it as the bears came up. Also he had heated some stones in a fire. When they told him what they wanted, he ordered them to go back. Now the bears were very angry, and the chief bear and his wife came up to fight, but Blood-Clot killed them by throwing hot stones down their throats.

Then he went down to the lodge of the bears and killed all, except one female who was about to become a mother. She pleaded so pitifully for her life, that he spared her. If he had not done this, there would have been no more bears in the world. The lodge of the bears was filled with dried meat and other property. Also all the young women of the camp were confined there. Blood-Clot gave all the property to the old women, and set free all the young women. The bears' lodge he gave to the old women.

"Now," said Blood-Clot, "I must go on my travels." He came to a camp and entered the lodge of some old women.

When these women saw what a fine young man he was, they said, "Why do you come here, among such old women? Why do you not go where there are younger people?"

"Well," said he, "give me some meat." The old women gave him some dried meat, but no fat. Then he said, "Why do you not give me some fat with my meat?"

"Hush!" said the women, "you must not speak so loud. There is a snake-lodge here, and the snakes take everything. They leave no fat for the people."

"Well," said Blood-Clot, "I will go over to the snake-lodge to eat."

"No, you must not do that," said the old women. "It is dangerous. They will surely kill you."

"Well," said he, "I must have some fat with my meat, even if they do kill me."

Then he entered the snake-lodge. He had his white rock knife ready. Now the snake, who was the head man in this lodge, had one horn on his head. He was lying with his head in the lap of a beautiful woman. He was asleep. By the fire was a bowl of berry-soup ready for the snake when he should wake. Blood-Clot seized the bowl and drank the soup.

Then the women warned him in whispers, "You must go away: you must not stay here."

But he said, "I want to smoke." So he took out his knife and cut off the head of the snake, saying as he did so, "Wake up! light a pipe! I want to smoke." Then with his knife he began to kill all the snakes. At last there was one snake who was about to become a mother, and she pleaded so pitifully for her life that she was allowed to go. From her descended all the snakes that are in the world. Now the lodge of the snakes was filled up with dried meat of every kind all with fat. Blood-Clot turned all this over to the people, the lodge and everything it contained. Then he said, "I must go away and visit other people."

So he started out. Some old women advised him to keep on the south side of the road, because it was dangerous the other way. But Blood-Clot paid no attention to their warning. As he was going along, a great windstorm struck him and at last carried him into the mouth of a great fish. This was a sucker-fish and the wind was its sucking. When he got into the stomach of the fish, he saw a great many people. Many of them were dead, but some were still alive. He said to the people, "Ah, there must be a heart somewhere here. We will have a dance." So he painted his face white, his eyes and mouth with black circles, and tied a white rock knife on his head, so that the point stuck up. Some rattles made of hoofs were also brought. Then the people started in to dance. For a while Blood-Clot sat making wing-motions with his hands, and singing songs. Then he stood up and danced, jumping up and down until the knife on his head struck the heart. Then he cut the heart down. Next he cut through between the ribs of the fish, and let all the people out.

Again Blood-Clot said he must go on his travels. Before starting, the people warned him, saying that after a while he would see a woman who was always challenging people to wrestle with her, but that he must not speak to her. He gave no heed to what they said, and, after he had gone a little way, he saw a woman who called him to come over. "No," said Blood-Clot. "I am in a hurry." However, at the fourth time the woman asked him to come over, he said, "Yes, but you must wait a little while, for I am tired. I wish to rest. When I have rested, I will come over and wrestle with you." Now, while he was resting, he saw many large knives sticking up from the ground almost hidden by straw. Then he knew that the woman killed the people she wrestled with by throwing them down on the knives.

When he was rested, he went over. The woman asked him to stand up in the place where he had seen the knives; but he said, "No, I am not quite ready. Let us play a little, before we begin." So he began to play with the woman, but quickly caught hold of her, threw her upon the knives, and cut her in two.

Blood-Clot took up his travels again, and after a while came to a camp where there were some old women. The old women told him that a little farther on he would come to a woman with a swing, but on no account must he ride with her. After a time he came to a place where he saw a swing on the bank of a swift stream. There was a woman swinging on it. He watched her a while, and saw that she killed people by swinging them out and dropping them into the water.

When he found this out, he came up to the woman. "You have a swing here; let me see you swing," he said.

"No," said the woman, "I want to see you swing."

"Well," said Blood-Clot, "but you must swing first"

"Well," said the woman, "Now I shall swing. Watch me. Then I shall see you do it." So the woman swung out over the stream. As she did this, he saw how it worked.

Then he said to the woman, "You swing again while I am getting ready;" but as the woman swung out this time, he cut the vine and let her drop into the water. This happened on Cut Bank Creek.

"Now," said Blood-Clot, "I have rid the world of all the monsters, I will go back to my old father and mother." So he climbed a high ridge, and returned to the lodge of the old couple. One day he said to them, "I shall go back to the place from whence I came. If you find that I have been killed, you must not be sorry, for then I shall go up into the sky and become the Smoking-Star." Then he went on and on, until he was killed by some Crow Indians on the war-path. His body was never found; but the moment he was killed, the Smoking-Star appeared in the sky, where we see it now.

Source: Adapted from "Blood Clot Boy," *Tales of the North American Indians.* Stith Thompson (Bloomington, IN: Indiana University Press, 1929), 108–113.

Chicken Girl Marries Sun Old Man: A Tewa Pueblo Cinderella

The younger daughter in the following tale told by the Tewa of Santa Clara Pueblo (New Mexico), like the heroine of "Cinderella," is mistreated by family members, finds a supernatural benefactor and is elevated in social status at the conclusion of the story. "Old Man" is a title of respect for Chicken Girl's suitor rather than an adjective designating age. The tale was collected in the 20th century; therefore, the plot is likely to be a Native American adaptation of the classic European folktale.

Once there were an old man and an old woman who had two daughters. They lived in the mountains and they had many mountain chickens.

One day the old man said to the younger daughter, "There is going to be a dance tonight. Your sister is going to the dance and you have to stay to take care of the chickens."

They left for the dance with the older daughter. They got there very early. The daughter was well dressed, and all the young men began to dance with her.

The younger daughter went out to feed the chickens. The rooster spoke to the girl and said, "Why don't you go to the dance also?"

"Because I have no shoes and no dress," she answered.

The rooster then said, "Strike me on the tail with a stick." The girl took a stick and struck the rooster on the tail and a beautiful pair of buckskin moccasins fell from the rooster's tail.

"Now strike me on the neck," said the rooster. The girl did so and a beautiful black shawl together with a belt fell from the rooster's neck.

"Put all that on," said the rooster.

"Now pull my ears," said the rooster. The girl did so and beautiful turquoise
earrings fell from the rooster's ears.

"Put them on," said the rooster.

"And now, pull me by the neck," said the rooster. She did so and red powder came out. "Powder your face with it," said the rooster. She did so. And now she was beautifully dressed.

"Now you can go to the dance," the rooster said. She gave the rooster wheat and water and left for the dance.

When the younger daughter was approaching the place where the dance was, a man came out from the woods with a wooden hoop. He was Sun Old Man [the personification of the sun, one of the principal deities of the Tewa].

"Where are you going?" Sun asked. She told him everything. She told him how her old parents had left her alone to take care of the chickens and how they had taken her older sister to the dance. She also told him how she had obtained the beautiful clothes from the rooster.

Then Sun said, "Now I am going to throw this hoop and wherever it falls there we two will jump." And he threw the hoop, they jumped and were very near the place where the dance was.

Then he said, "Now I am going to throw the hoop again and we will jump again." And he threw the hoop again and again they jumped and were at the door of the dance house.

Sun then said, "We have arrived. Now I will throw the hoop again and we will jump and enter the house from the north." He did so and they jumped right into the dance house from the north.

The others saw them and wondered who they were. The older sister said to her parents, "I think it is that stubborn one we left at home."

"No," said the mother, "it cannot be she."

"Yes it is," said the older daughter; "I know it is my sister."

Sun old man and the younger sister sat down near the stairs. They stayed there a little while and everybody looked at them. The older sister went over and recognized her younger sister. Her younger sister asked her to sit near her. She refused. She went away.

She was jealous. They all began to talk about them. Then they drank and ate. The dancers came out. And Sun and the younger sister also danced. And since she was so beautifully dressed all were jealous of her. And the parents were angry because she had left the chickens and come to the dance.

Sun old man said at last, "I must go now."

"I will go with you," said the girl. They left the house. All were looking at them and wondering who they were.

When they were outside Sun said, "I will throw the hoop and we will jump where it lands." He threw the hoop and they jumped. They were near the girl's home.

Again he said, "I am going to throw the hoop again." He did and then they reached the house.

A third time he threw the hoop and it landed on top of the house. They jumped on the roof. There the girl began to weep and said, "Now I am going to be punished when my parents return." But Sun gave her a pine seed to sow there on the roof. She sowed the seed and immediately a pine began to grow.

"Take all your chickens and get up on the pine tree," said Sun. She gathered her chickens and got on the tree. And Sun disappeared and the tree grew and grew. By the time the parents reached home the tree had reached halfway up to the sky.

They called the people to see it. And the mother saw her daughter up there on the tree and began to cry. "It is all my fault," she cried out. "It is because I told her I didn't love her and that she was dirty and stubborn."

And the girl replied from the tree. "Yes; it was because you were so mean with me. I am going away with a man."

The parents then wanted to cut down the tree. The people went for axes. And they began to cut on the side of the east. And this was the side of the sun. And the tree soon fell toward the sun. And the chickens all fell along the mountains where they still live.

The girl fell toward the east at a spring where Sun lives. And there she married Sun Old Man, and lives with him.

Source: Adapted from "The Chicken Girl Marries Old Sun Man," Aurelio M. Espinosa. *Journal of American Folklore,* 49 (1936): 69–133, pp. 111–112.

The Deserted Children

Residing in northern Montana, the Gros Ventres pursued a traditional Plains lifestyle based on nomadic buffalo hunting, like the Arapaho to whom they are related. Two widely distributed Native American cultural principles are central to the following tale. The first is the imperative of generosity and mutual support within a social group, particularly the family. The second is that extraordinary human power commonly emanates from the animal world. Therefore, the siblings in the following narrative are transformed from victims of human oppressors to conquering avengers by their alliances with a series of animal helpers.

There was a camp. All the children went off to play. They went to some distance. Then one man said, "Let us abandon the children. Lift the ends of your tent-poles and travois when you go, so that there will be no trail." Then the people went off.

After a time the oldest girl among the children sent the others back to the camp to get something to eat. The children found the camp gone, the fires out, and only ashes about. They cried, and wandered about at random. The oldest girl said, "Let us go toward the river."

They found a trail leading across the river, and forded the river there. Then one of the girls found a tent-pole. As they went along, she cried, "My mother, here is your tent-pole."

"Bring my tent-pole here!" shouted an old woman loudly from out of the timber. The children went toward her.

They found that she was an old woman who lived alone. They entered her tent. At night they were tired. The old woman told them all to sleep with their heads toward the fire. Only one little girl who had a small brother pretended to sleep, but did not. The old woman watched if all were asleep. Then she put her foot in the fire. It became red hot. Then she pressed it down on the throat of one of the children, and burned through the child's throat. Then she killed the next one and the next one.

The little girl jumped up, saying, "My grandmother, let me live with you and work for you. I will bring wood and water for you." Then the old woman allowed her and her little brother to live. "Take these out," she said.

Then the little girl, carrying her brother on her back, dragged out the bodies of the other children. Then the old woman sent her to get wood. The little girl brought back a load of cottonwood. When she brought it, the old woman said, "That is not the kind of wood I use. Throw it out. Bring another load."

The little girl went out and got willow-wood. She came back, and said, "My grandmother, I have a load of wood."

"Throw it in," said the old woman. The little girl threw the wood into the tent.

The old woman said, "That is not the kind of wood I use. Throw it outside. Now go get wood for me."

Then the little girl brought birch-wood, then cherry, then sagebrush; but the old woman always said, "That is not the kind of wood I use," and sent her out again.

The little girl went. She cried and cried. Then a bird came to her and told her, "Bring her ghost-ropes for she is a ghost." Then the little girl brought some of these plants, which grow on willows.

The old woman said, "Throw in the wood which you have brought." The little girl threw it in. Then the old woman was glad. "You are my good grand-daughter," she said.

Then the old woman sent the little girl to get water. The little girl brought her river-water, then rain-water, then spring-water; but the old woman always told her, "That is not the kind of water I use. Spill it!"

Then the bird told the little girl, "Bring her foul, stagnant water, which is muddy and full of worms. That is the only kind she drinks." The little girl got the water, and when she brought it the old woman was glad.

Then the little boy said that he needed to go out doors. "Well, then, go out with your brother, but let half of your robe remain inside of the tent while you hold him." Then the girl took her little brother out, leaving half of her robe inside the tent. When she was outside, she stuck an awl in the ground. She hung her robe on this, and, taking her little brother, fled.

The old woman called, "Hurry!"

Then the awl answered, "My grandmother, my little brother is not yet ready."

Again the old woman said, "Now hurry!"

Then the awl answered again, "My little brother is not ready."

Then the old woman said, "Come in now; else I will go outside and kill you." She started to go out, and stepped on the awl.

The little girl and her brother fled, and came to a large river. An animal with two horns lay there. It said, "Louse me." The little boy loused it. Its lice were frogs. "Catch four, and crack them with your teeth," said the Water-monster. The boy had on a necklace of plum-seeds. Four times the girl cracked a seed. She made the monster think that her brother had cracked one of its lice. Then the Water-monster said, "Go between my horns, and do not open your eyes until we have crossed." Then he went under the surface of the water. He came up on the other side. The children got off and went on.

The old woman was pursuing the children, saying, "I will kill you. You cannot escape me by going to the sky or by entering the ground." She came to the river. The monster had returned, and was lying at the edge of the water.

"Louse me," it said. The old woman found a frog. "These dirty lice! I will not put them into my mouth!" she said, and threw it into the river. She found three more, and threw them away. Then she went on the Water-monster. He went under the surface of the water, remained there, drowned her, and ate her. The children went on.

At last they came to the camp of the people who had deserted them. They came to their parents' tent. "My mother, here is your little son," the girl said.

"I did not know that I had a son," their mother said. They went to their father, their uncle, and their grandfather. They all said, "I did not know I had a son," "I did not know I had a nephew," "I did not know I had a grandson." Then a man said, "Let us tie them face to face, and hang them in a tree and leave them."

Then they tied them together, hung them in a tree, put out all the fires, and left them. A small dog with sores all over his body, his mouth, and his eyes, pretended to be sick and unable to move, and lay on the ground. He kept a little fire between his legs, and had hidden a knife. The people left the dog lying. When they had all gone off, the dog went to the children, climbed the tree, cut the ropes, and freed them. The little boy cried and cried. He felt bad about what the people had done.

Then many buffalo came near them. "Look at the buffalo, my brother," said the girl. The boy looked at the buffalo, and they fell dead. The girl wondered how they might cut them up. "Look at the meat, my younger brother," she said. The boy looked at the dead buffalo, and the meat was all cut up. Then she told him to look at the meat, and when he looked at it, the meat was dried. Then they had much to eat, and the dog became well again. The girl sat down on the pile of buffalo-skins, and they were all dressed. She folded them together, sat on them, and there was a tent. Then she went out with the dog and looked for sticks. She brought dead branches, broken tent-poles, and rotten wood. "Look at the tent-poles," she said to her brother. When he looked, there were large straight tent-poles, smooth and good. Then the girl tied three together at the top, and stood them up, and told her brother to look at the tent. He looked, and a large fine tent stood there. Then she told him to go inside and look about him. He went in and looked. Then the tent was filled with property, and there were beds for them, and a bed also for the dog. The dog was an old man. Then the girl said, "Look at the antelopes running, my brother." The boy looked, and the antelopes fell dead. He looked at them again, and the meat was cut up and the skins taken off.

Then the girl made fine dresses of the skins for her brother and herself and the dog. Then she called as if she were calling for dogs, and four bears came loping to her. "You watch that pile of meat, and you this one," she said to each one of the bears. The bears went to the meat and watched it. Then the boy looked at the woods and there was a corral full of fine painted horses. Then the children lived at this place, the same place where they had been tied and abandoned. They had very much food and much property.

Then a man came and saw their tent and the abundance they had, and went back and told the people. Then the people were told, "Break camp and move to the children for we are without food." Then they broke camp and traveled, and came to the children. The women went to take meat, but the bears drove them away. The girl and her brother would not come out of the tent. Not even the dog would come out.

Then the girl said, "I will go out and bring a wife for you, my brother, and for the dog, and a husband for myself." Then she went out, and went to the camp and selected two pretty girls and one good-looking young man, and told them to come with her. She took them into the tent, and the girls sat down by the boy and the old man, and the man by her. Then they gave them fine clothing, and married them. Then the sister told her brother, "Go outside and look at the camp." The boy went out and looked at the people, and they all fell dead.

Source: "The Deserted Children," Tales of the North American Indians, Stith Thompson (Bloomington: Indiana University Press, 1929), 174–178.

Montezuma and the Salt Woman

This culture hero tale developed in the centuries following the conquest of San Juan and the other Tewa Pueblos of New Mexico by the Spanish. Among the cultural borrowings found in the narrative are Our Lady of Lourdes (who plays the role usually filled by Sun in Tewa myth), Christ, and Montezuma. Montezuma, who brings technological, sacred, and social gifts to his people, is a synthesis of Native American culture hero and Christian messiah. The tale illustrates the ways in which cultures are able to maintain ties to indigenous world views while incorporating outside influences in situations of cultural contact.

A long time ago, long before the time of bows and arrows, there lived in the Pueblo of San Gabriel near San Juan, Salinas, the mother of Montezuma. Salinas lived with her mother in the pueblo.

They were very poor and they were despised by everybody. At that time there was no shame. Everybody was naked.

One year there was lots of pinyon nuts and deer and mountain lions. The Indians went out on a hunt. When the announcers called the Indians out for the hunt, Salinas and her mother went out also. They were very poor and wanted to get meat to eat. When Salinas went along, some of the Indians began to make fun of her because she was a woman going hunting. She got angry and covered herself with a skin.

When they were hunting, Salinas and her mother went separate from the rest. Nobody wanted to go with them. Then they began to gather pinyon. And there where Salinas was alone with her mother a beautiful lady appeared to them. She was Our Lady of Lourdes. She told Salinas not to be frightened. Then she asked her, "What are you doing here?"

Salinas told her she was hunting there with her mother and that they had seen lots of pinyon and were gathering some. "The people of the pueblo are envious of us," she said.

Our Lady of Lourdes then took some pinyon and gave Salinas one pinyon to eat. Then she said to Salinas, "You will be the mother of a beautiful child." And she disappeared.

Salinas at once became pregnant. She began to cry and went home with her mother.

As soon as she reached the pueblo the Indians came out to taunt her. They called her poor, dirty, and ugly. And after a while they all began to notice that she was heavy with child and then they insulted her and called her vile names.

One day, Salinas and her mother were out hunting. Salinas threw a stone at a rabbit and just then she gave birth to a beautiful child.

She called to her mother and said, "Mother, I don't know what is happening to me." The mother arrived and picked up the child. Then she put some water in a large stone jar, put some herbs into it and Salinas bathed twice and became well. Then the grandmother bathed the child.

When they returned to the pueblo, all wondered at the beauty of the child. When he was six months old he was very beautiful.

Then one of the Principals [council members] of the pueblo went to see the child and he asked Salinas, "Where did you steal that child?"

"I didn't steal it," said Salinas. "It is my own child."

This Indian went and told everything to the Governor [head of the village council]. The chief men were greatly surprised. They called a meeting and discussed the matter. Some wanted to kill Salinas and her mother. They wanted to stone them to death in order to get hold of the boy. But they finally decided not to kill them.

When the child was about a year old he could run around and talk like a grown person. And one day he was at the door of his mother's house when he heard the announcer calling the Indians to a hunt.

The child ran to his mother Salinas and asked her, "Mother, mother, tell me what that man is saying." His mother explained that he was calling the Indians to a hunt. She said they were going to hunt rabbits, deer, and other animals.

"Where do they hunt?" asked the young Montezuma. He was Montezuma, the Indian God. Montezuma is like Christ. He and Christ are the same thing.

The mother told him that the Indians hunted in the mountains. "There they fight with bears, take rabbits out of their holes with sticks, and kill hares with stones," she told him.

"That is not the best way to hunt," said the child. "I am going to think of a better way." And he asked his mother and grandmother to allow him to go hunting with the men. He went along.

While hunting some of the Indians liked him and others didn't. Some said bad words to him and called him a bastard. He was a very smart child. He saw everything the hunters did but never said anything. He saw them kill rabbits with stones and by taking them out of their holes with sticks, and deer by chasing them over cliffs where they would fall and be caught.

When they returned from the hunt he called his mother and said to her, "I want you to take me to where I can find some reeds to make bows and arrows." His mother took him to a place where there were lots of reeds and small willows. The child Montezuma took some and began to peel them nicely. Then he straightened them with his teeth. He cut them about two feet long and made points on them. On the other ends he made a cut with a sharp flint. Then when the arrows were finished he took a piece of willow and peeled it nicely for a bow. For a string he got some palmilla leaves, chewed them, and twisted them around into a strong string for the bow. Now he had a bow and arrows. Then he showed his mother how he was going to kill rabbits and deer. And he shot away a few arrows.

They came back home. The next time the announcer called the people for a hunt young Montezuma ran out and said, "I am going out to kill rabbits and hares." He was just a little over a year old.

All the men began to laugh. "How can you kill rabbits, you little brat?" they said.

He said nothing, but went with them. He went with his mother and grandmother. They were hunting, separated from the rest. Soon he saw a man bent over a rabbit hole taking the rabbit out with a stick. Young Montezuma thought it was some animal and shot at it. He hit the man in the leg and the man died. Then they got scared and went home. But on the way he killed many rabbits and hares and they took them home. When they reached home they put out the rabbit meat to dry. Everybody saw that they had plenty of meat. The others killed very few rabbits and wondered how the boy had killed so many.

The Indians found the dead hunter and took him home. They did not know how he had died. They never suspected that young Montezuma had killed him by mistake. And the young child went out hunting many times, but always alone. And he always returned with plenty of rabbits and other animals. And finally the Governor wanted to know how the young hunter killed his rabbits. Everybody was talking about the young man and his mother. They said they always had dry meat at home. The Governor sent some of the chiefs to the house of Salinas.

"We want to know how you always have plenty of meat when the rest of us have hardly any," they said to her.

"It is my boy that kills the rabbit and hare and deer," she said.

"But how does he do it?" they asked.

Then the boy appeared and said to them, "Please don't do anything to my mother. I will show you how I kill all those animals."

He took out his bow and arrows. And to show them how to use the bow and arrows he saw a bird flying by and he shot at it and killed it. Then he took the feathers and began to put them on the arrows. "This way they will fly better," he said. All the people were surprised.

The Governor called a meeting of all the people at the kiva and asked the boy to come also. He said they could all learn much from the boy.

When all the people were gathered at the kiva [ceremonial chamber] the Governor came in with young Montezuma and his mother and his grandmother. And some of the people were still jealous and hated them. But the Governor told them that the boy was going to teach them how to hunt. The boy stood on a stone in the middle of the kiva and spoke. He spoke for a long time and told them how to make bows and arrows and showed them how to shoot with them. He showed them his own bow and arrows.

All marveled at his knowledge and after that everybody liked him. They did not talk about his mother any more. They all left and started to make bows and arrows. And he taught them to put feathers on the arrows and told them also to put flint points on them when they wanted to kill deer and bear. Then he showed them how to put poison in the arrow points by boiling certain herbs.

After that the Indians learned to hunt with arrows and they always had plenty of meat to eat. Then young Montezuma showed them how to plant corn and melons and other fruits. Then they began to plant corn and keep it for the winter. Then he taught them the Indian dances and everything else that they had to do. He told them to pray for rain to the sun and the moon. And by the time he taught them everything there was to know, he was fifteen years old. Then they elected him Governor of all the Tewa pueblos in the Rio Grande Valley. At that time there was no shame and all went about naked. But Montezuma thought it was better for the Indians to wear clothes and moccasins and he taught them to make them. Then he taught them to kill white eagles with which the men could adorn themselves for the dances.

After they had learned everything he called them together one day and ordered a great festival. They had dances and games and races. And when the day was over he told them to adore the magnetic stone so that they would fare well in all their undertakings. And Tewas from all parts of the country came to the festival and there all learned everything. And the festival lasted fifteen days. He taught all the Tewas the dances and told them when to have each dance. He told them to have the bison dance in January and the deer dance in February. He taught them to dance the Matachines.

Then after the festival all the Tewas went back to their pueblos and organized their dances and their way of living.

Montezuma then went out to all the Tewa pueblos to see that everything he had taught them was done. And wherever he went the Tewas received him with great honor. And when he stepped on the rocks his tracks remained forever. Even when he sat on a rock his buttocks remained impressed there. But some became envious. And he knew it and said he was going to abandon the Tewas. But before leaving he danced the Matachines. He was the Monarca. And only the pueblos of San Juan and Santa Clara learned the Matachines. He never married. And he brought the *aguelos (abuelos,* "grandfathers" in the Matachines Dance) from the mountains. And then he told his people that white people would come some day to rule over them.

During the festival Salinas, the mother of Montezuma, boiled some meat and did not put any salt in it. A man who was eating some of it said, "This meat has no salt." Then Salinas blew her nose and pretending she was putting mucus into the meat she put a little salt in it.

The man did not eat the meat. He said loudly, "What a dirty thing to do !" And it was really salt. And after this the Indians of San Juan and the other Tewa pueblos had to go to a lake for salt, the lake called Laguna Salina. And at that moment all began to be ashamed and began to cover their nakedness.

Montezuma then told them that Salinas, his mother, would go far away from them. And he went and made some very long whistles and with them he called all the animals. He spoke to all the animals in their different languages. Then he told the Indians that he was going to leave. He said that he was going to Mexico and that those who wished could follow him. He said goodbye and left. A few Indians followed him and those are the Indians that are well off today. Those that remained were the stubborn and ignorant Indians. The animals went ahead. Montezuma left at dawn. He went to a lake above Santa Fe and there he still lives enchanted. He lives in an enchanted house and there are always singing and dancing there. And before leaving Montezuma told the Indians that he would return some day at sunrise. And the Indians that went with him are those from Oklahoma and Mexico. They are now in a prosperous condition and live well. And those that stayed have not got along well.

The grandmother of Montezuma went to Agua Fria and there she became a stone. And there the Indians go to adore the stone. And Salinas, the mother of Montezuma, went to Salinas near Terreros.

Source: Adapted from "Montezuma and Salt Woman," Aurelio M. Espinosa. *Journal of American Folklore,* 49 (1936): 69–133, pp. 98–101.

Raven

Trickster figures pose one of the great contradictions in the world's folk narratives. Like Raven they commonly take an animal form, yet behave like humans. They transform the world around them and the beings that inhabit it; yet, they willfully exploit and destroy in the next moment. In this case, Raven is less a benevolent Creator with a master plan than a character who uses his wiles to accomplish his own immediate purposes. That a figure given the responsibility of shaping the world should deviate so from the norm seems puzzling until we consider that invention demands deviation from the ordinary, what has been labeled "lateral thinking." Along with the overall theme of how surface deviousness may be genius in disguise, the following myth of the adventures of the trickster hero Raven explains the origins of features of the environment that are central to the lifestyle of the maritime Tlingit of the Northwest. See the Inuit myth Raven Befriends the Human Race *for a different perspective on Raven.*

No one knows just how the story of Raven really begins, so each starts from the point where he does know it. Here it was always begun in this way. When Raven was born, his father the Creator tried to instruct him and train him in every way and, after he grew up, told him he would give him strength to make a world. After trying in all sorts of ways Raven finally succeeded. Then there was no light in this world, but it was told him that far up the Nass River was a large house in which some one kept light just for himself.

Raven thought over all kinds of plans for getting this light into the world and finally he hit on a good one. The rich man living there had a daughter, and he thought, "I will make myself very small and drop into the water in the form of a small piece of dirt." The girl swallowed this dirt and became pregnant. When her time was completed, they made a hole for her, as was customary, and lined it with rich furs of all sorts. But the child did not wish to be born on those fine things. Then its grandfather felt sad and said, "What do you think it would be best to put into that hole? Shall we put in moss?" So they put moss inside and the baby was born on it. Its eyes were very bright and moved around rapidly.

Round bundles of varying shapes and sizes hung about on the walls of the house. When the child became a little larger it crawled around back of the people weeping continually, and as it cried it pointed to the bundles. This lasted many days. Then its grandfather said, "Give my grandchild what he is crying for. Give him that one hanging on the end. That is the bag of stars." So the child played with this, rolling it about on the floor back of the people, until suddenly he let it go up through the smoke hole. It went straight up into the sky and the stars scattered out of it, arranging themselves as you now see them. That was what he went there for.

Some time after this he began crying again, and he cried so much that it was thought he would die. Then his grandfather said, "Untie the next one and give it to him." He played and played with it around behind his mother. After a while he let that go up through the smoke hole also, and there was the big moon.

Now just one thing more remained, the box that held the daylight, and he cried for that. His eyes turned around and showed different colors, and the people began thinking that he must be something other than an ordinary baby. But it always happens that a grandfather loves his grandchild just as he does his own daughter, so the grandfather said, "Untie the last thing and give it to him." His grandfather felt very sad when he gave this to him. When the child had this in his hands, he uttered the raven cry, "Gâ," and flew out with it through the smoke hole. Then the person from whom he had stolen it said, "That old Raven has gotten all of my things.

Journeying on, Raven was told of another place, where a man had an everlasting spring of water. This man was named Petrel (a type of sea bird). Raven wanted this water because there was none to drink in this world, but Petrel always slept by his spring, and he had a cover over it so as to keep it all to himself. Then Raven came in and said to him, "My brother-in-law, I have just come to see you. How are you?" He told Petrel of all kinds of things that were happening outside, trying to induce him to go out to look at them, but Petrel was too smart for him and refused.

When night came, Raven said, "I am going to sleep with you, brother-in-law." So they went to bed, and toward morning Raven heard Petrel sleeping very soundly. Then Raven went over to Petrel's spring, took off the cover and began drinking. After he had drunk up almost all of the water, Petrel came in and saw him. Then Raven flew straight up, crying "Gâ."

Before he got through the smoke hole, however, Petrel said, "My spirits up the smoke hole, catch him." So Raven stuck there, and Petrel put pitch wood on the fire under him so as to make a quantity of smoke. Raven was white before that time, but the smoke made him of the color you find him today. Still he did not drop the water. When the smoke-hole spirits let him go, he flew around the nearest point and rubbed himself all over so as to clear off as much of the soot as possible.

This happened somewhere about the Nass River, and afterwards he started up this way. First he let some water fall from his mouth and made the Nass. By and by he spit more out and made all the other large rivers. The small drops that came out of his mouth made the small salmon creeks.

After this Raven went on again and came to a large town where there were people who had never seen daylight. They were out catching smelt in the darkness when he came to the bank opposite, and he asked them to take him across but they would not. Then he said to them, "If you don't come over I will have daylight break on you."

But they answered, "Where are you from? Do you come from far up the Nass where lives the man who has daylight?" At this Raven opened his box just a little and shed so great a light on them that they were nearly thrown down. He shut it quickly, but they quarreled with him so much across the creek that he became angry and opened the box completely. Then the sun flew up into the sky. Then those people who had sea-otter or fur-seal skins, or the skins of any other sea animals, went into the ocean, while those who had land-otter, bear, or marten skins, or the skins of any other land-animals, went into the woods. becoming the animals whose skins they wore.

Raven came to another place where a crowd of boys were throwing fat at one another. When they hit him with a piece he swallowed it. The boys became scared, ran away, and threw more fat at him. He consumed all in this way, and started on again.

After a while he came to an abandoned camp where lay a piece of jade half buried in the ground, on which some design had been pecked. This he dug up. Far out in the bay he saw a large spring salmon jumping about and wanted to get it but did not know how. Then he stuck his stone into the ground and put eagle down upon the head designed thereon. The next time the salmon jumped, he said, "See here, spring salmon jumping out there, do you know what this green stone is saying to you? It is saying, 'You thing with dirty, filthy back, you thing with dirty, filthy gills, come ashore here.'"

Just then the big spring salmon also started to come ashore. Raven took a piece of wild celery, and, when the salmon did come ashore, he struck it with this and killed it. Because Raven made this jade talk to the salmon, people have since made stone axes, picks, and spears out of it. Then, Raven, carrying along the spring salmon, got all kinds of birds, little and big, as his servants.

When he came to a good place to cook his fish he said to all of them, "Here, you young fellows, go after skunk cabbage. We will bury this in the ground and roast it." After they had brought it down, however, he said, "I don't want any of that. It is dirty, and I will not use it. Go back and pass over two mountains." While they were gone, Raven put all of the salmon except for one fat piece into the skunk cabbage and buried it in the fire. Before they returned, he dug this up and ate it, after which he put the bones back into the fire and covered them up.

When the birds at last came back he said to them, "I have been across two mountains myself. Now it is time to dig it up. Dig it out." Then all crowded around the fire and dug, but, when they got it up, there was nothing there but bones.

By and by the birds dressed one another in different ways so that they might be named from their dress. They tied the hair of the blue jay up high with a string, and they added a long tail to, another crested bird. Then they named one another.

Now Raven started off with the piece of salmon belly and came to a place where Bear and his wife lived. He entered and said, "My cousin, is this you?" The piece of salmon he had buried behind a little point.

Then Bear told him to sit down and said, "I will roast some dry salmon for you." So he began to roast it. After it was done, he set a dish close to the fire and slit the back of his hands with a knife so as to let grease run out for Raven to eat on his salmon. After he had fixed the salmon, he cut a piece of flesh out from in front of his thighs and put it into the dish. That is why bears are not fat in that place.

Now Raven wanted to give a dinner to Bear in return, so he, too, took out a piece of fish, roasted it, set out the dish Bear had used, close to the fire and slit up the back of his hand, thinking that grease would run out of it. But instead nothing but white bubbles came forth. Although he knew he could not do it, he tried in every way.

Starting on again, Raven came to a place where many people were encamped fishing. They used nothing but fat for bait. He entered a house and asked what they used for bait. They said "Fat."

Then he said, "Let me see you put enough on your hooks for bait," and he noticed carefully how they baited and handled their hooks. The next time they went out, he walked off behind a point and went under water to get this bait. Now they got bites and pulled up quickly, but there was nothing on their hooks. This continued for a long time. The next time they went out they felt the thing again, but one man among them who knew just how fish bite, jerked at the right moment and felt that he had caught something. The line went around in the water very fast. They pulled away, however, until they got Raven under the canoe, and he kicked against it very hard. All at once his nose came off, and they pulled it up. When they landed, they took it to the chief's house and said, "We have caught a wonderful thing. It must be the nose of the God of the Sea." So they took it, put eagle down on it, and hung it up on the wall.

After that, Raven came ashore at the place where he had been in the habit of going down, got a lot of spruce gum and made a new nose out of it. Then he drew a hat down over his face and went to the town. Beginning at the nearer end he went through the houses saying "I wonder in what house are the people who caught that Sea God's nose." After he had gone halfway, he entered the chief's house and inquired, "Do you know where are the people who caught that GonaqAdê't's nose?"

They answered, "There it is on the wall." Then he said, "Bring it here. Let me examine it." So they gave it to him. "This is great," he said, and he put up his hat to examine it.

"Why," said he, "this house is dark. You ought to take off the smoke-hole cover. Let some one run up and take it off so that I can see." But, as soon as they removed it, he put the nose in its place, cried "Gâ," and flew away. They did not find out who he was.

Going thence, Raven saw a number of deer walking around on the beach, with a great deal of fat hanging out through their noses. As he passed one of these, he said, "Brother, you better blow your nose. Lots of dirt is hanging out of it." When the deer would not do this, Raven came close to him, wiped his nose and threw the fat by his own side. Calling out, "Just for the Raven," he swallowed it.

Now Raven formed a certain plan. He got a small canoe and began paddling along the beach saying, "I wonder who is able to go along with me."

Mink came down and said, "How am I?" and Raven said, "What can you do?"

Said Mink, "When I go to camp with my friends, I make a bad smell in their noses with my musk glands. How about that?"

But Raven said, "I guess not. You might make a hole in my canoe," so he went along farther. The various animals and birds would come down and say, "How am I?" but he did not even listen.

After some time Deer ran down to him, saying, "How am I?"

Then he answered, "Come this way. Come this way." Finally Raven came ashore and said to Deer, "Don't hurt yourself." By and by Raven said " Not very far from here my father has been making a canoe. Let us go there and look at it."

Then Raven brought him to a large valley. He took very many pieces of dried wild celery and laid them across the valley, covering them with moss. Said Raven, "Watch me, watch me." Repeating this over and over he went straight across on it, for he is light. Afterwards he said to Deer, "Now you come and try it. It will not break," and he crossed once more. "You better try it now," he said. "Come on over." Deer did so, but, as he was on the way, he broke through the bridge and smashed his head to pieces at the bottom. Then Raven went down, walked all over him, and said to himself, "I wonder where I better start, at the root of his tail, at the eyes, or at the heart." He ate very fast.

When he started on from this place, he began crying, "Deer! Deer!," and the fowls asked him, "What has become of your friend, "Deer?"

"Some one has taken him and pounded him on the rocks, and I have been walking around and hopping around since he died."

By and by he came to a certain cliff and saw a door in it swing open. He got behind a point quickly, for he knew that here lived the woman who has charge of the falling and rising of the tide. Far out Raven saw some kelp, and, going out to this, he climbed down on it to the bottom of the sea and gathered up a number of small sea urchins that were lying about there. He brought these ashore and began eating, making a great gulping noise as he did so. Meanwhile the woman inside of the cliff kept mocking him saying, "During what tide did he get those things?"

While Raven was eating Mink came along, and Raven said, "Come here. Come here." Then he went on eating.

And the woman again said, "On what tide did you get those sea urchins you are making so much noise about?"

"That is not your business," answered Raven. "Keep quiet or I will stick their spines all over your buttocks." Finally, Raven became angry, seized the knife he was cutting up the sea urchins with and slit up the front of the cliff out of which she spoke. Then he ran in, knocked her down and began sticking the spines into her.

"Stop, Raven, stop," she cried, "the tide will begin to go down."

So he said to his servant, Mink, "Run outside and see how far down the tide has gone." Mink ran out and said, "It is just beginning to go down." The next time he came in he said, "The tide is still farther down." The third time he said, "The tide is lower yet. It has uncovered everything on the beach."

Then Raven said to the old woman, "Are you going to let the tide rise and fall again regularly through the months and years?"

She answered "Yes."

After the tide had gone down very far he and his servant went out. He said to Mink, "The thing that will be your food from now on is the sea urchin. You will live on it." The tide now goes up and down because he treated this woman so.

Leaving this place, Raven came to another where he saw something floating not far from shore, though it never came any nearer. He assembled all kinds of fowl. Toward evening he looked at the object and saw that it resembled fire. So he told a chicken hawk that had a very long bill to fly out to it, saying, "Be very brave. If you get some of that fire, do not let go of it." The chicken hawk reached the place, seized some fire and started back as fast as it could fly, but by the time it got the fire to Raven its bill was burned off. That is why its bill is short. Then Raven took some red cedar, and some white stones called which are found on the beach, and he put fire into them so that it could be found ever afterward all over the world.

After he had finished distributing the fire he started on again and came to a town where there were many people. He saw what looked like a large animal far off on the ocean with fowl all over the top of it. He wondered very much what it was and at last thought of a way of finding out. He said to one of his friends, "Go up and cut a cane for me." Then he carved this cane so as to resemble two tentacles of a devil fish. He said, "No matter how far off a thing is, this cane will always reach it."

Afterward he went to the middle of the town and said, "I am going to give a feast. My mother is dead, and I am going to beat the drums this evening. I want all of the people to come in and see me." In the evening he assembled all of the people, and they began to beat drums. Then he held the cane in his hands and moved it around horizontally, testing it. He kept saying "Up, up, up." He said, "I have never given any feast to mark my mother's passing, and it is time I did it, but I have nothing with which to give a feast. Therefore I made this cane, and I am going to give a feast for my mother with this wonderful thing."

Then he got the people all down on the beach and extended his cane toward the mysterious object until it reached it. And he began to draw it in little by little, saying to the people, "Sing stronger all the time." When it struck land, a wave burst it open. It was an everlasting house, containing everything that was to be in the waters of the world. He told the people to carry up fish and they did so. If one had a canoe, he filled it; if he had a box, he filled that; and those that had canoes also boiled eulachon in them. Since then they have known how to boil them. With all of these things Raven gave the feast for his mother.

After this was over he thought up a plot against the killer whales and sent an invitation to them. Then he told each of his people to make a cane that would reach very much above his head. So, when the killer whales came in and inquired, "What do the people use those canes for that extend up over their heads?" he replied, "They stick them down into their heads." They asked him several times, and he replied each time in the same way.

After a while one of the whales said, "Suppose we try it."

Raven was glad to hear that and said, "All right, we will try it with you people, but the people I have invited must not look when I put a cane into anyone's head." Then he went away and whittled a number of sticks until they were very sharp. After that he laid all of the killer whales on the beach at short distances apart, and again he told them not to look up while he was showing one how it was done. Then he took a hammer or maul and drove his sticks into the necks of these whales one after the other so that they died. But the last one happened to look up, saw what was being done, and jumped into the ocean.

Now Raven and another person started to boil out the killer-whales' grease, and the other man had more than he. So Raven dreamed a dream which informed him that a lot of people were coming to fight with him, and, when such people really did make their appearance, he told his companion to run out. After he had done so, Raven quickly drank all the latter's grease. By and by, however, the man returned, threw Raven into a grease box, and shut him in, and started to tie it up with a strong rope.

Then Raven called out, "My brother, do not tie the box up very strongly. Tie it with a piece of straw such as our forefathers used to use." The man did so, after which he took the box up on a high cliff and kicked it over. Then

Raven, breaking the straw, flew out, crying "Gâ." When he got to the other side of the point, he alighted and began wiping himself.

Raven once went to a certain place outside of here (Sitka) in his canoe. It was calm there, but he began rocking the canoe up and down with his feet until he had made a great many waves. Therefore, there are many waves there now even when it is calm outside, and a canoe going in there always gets lost.

By and by Raven came to a sea gull standing at the mouth of a creek and said to it, "What are you sitting in my way for? Fly out and see if you can bring in a herring."

After they had quarreled over it for a long time, the gull became angry, flew out to sea, and brought back a big herring. He lighted near Raven and laid the herring beside him, but, when Raven tried to get it, he gulped it down. In another direction from the sea gull Raven saw a large heron and went over to it. He said to the heron, "Sea gull is calling you Big-long-legs-always-walking-upon-the beach."

Then, although the heron did not reply, he went back to the sea gull and said, "Do you know what that heron is saying about you? He says that you have a big stomach and get your red eyes by sitting on the beach always looking out on the ocean for something to eat."

Then he went back to the heron and said to it, "When I meet a man of my own size, I always kick him just below the stomach. That fellow is talking too much about you. Go over, and I will help you thrash him." So the heron went over toward the sea gull, and, when he came close to it, Raven said, "Kick him just under his stomach." He did so, and the big herring came out. Then Raven swallowed it quickly saying, "Just for the Raven."

Next Raven came to a town where lived a man called Fog-on-the-Salmon. He wanted to marry this man's daughter because he always had plenty of salmon. He had charge of that place. So he married her, and they dried quantities of salmon, after which they filled many animal stomachs with salmon eggs. Then he loaded his canoe and started home. He put all of the fish eggs into the bow. On the way it became stormy, and they could not make much headway, so he became tired and threw his paddles into the bow, exclaiming to his wife, "Now you paddle!" Then the salmon eggs shouted out, "It is very hard to be in stomachs. Hand the paddles here and let me pull." So the salmon eggs did, and, when they reached home, Raven took all of them and dumped them overboard. But the dried salmon he carried up. That is why people now use dried salmon and do not care much for salmon eggs.

Journeying on, Raven came to a seal sitting on the edge of a rock, and he wanted to get it, but the seal jumped into the ocean. Farther on he came to a town and went behind a tree to watch. After a while a man came out, took a little club from a certain place where he kept it in concealment, and said to it, "My little club, do you see, that seal out there? Go and get it." So it went out and brought the little seal ashore. The club was hanging to its neck. Then the man took it up and said, "My little club, you have done well," after which he put it back in its place and returned to the town.

Raven saw where it was kept, but first he went to the town and spoke kindly to the owner of it. In the night, however, when every one was asleep, he went back to the club, carried it behind a point and said to it, "See here, my little club, you see that seal out in the water. Go and get it." But the club would not go because it did not know him. After he had tried to get it to go for some time, he became angry and said to it, "Little club, don't you see that seal out there?" He kept striking it against a rock until he broke it in pieces.

Now he went on from this place and camped by himself. There he saw a large sculpin trying to get ashore below him, and he said to it, "My uncle's son, come ashore here. Come way up. One time, when you and I were going along in our uncle's canoe we fell into the water. So come up a little farther." Raven was very hungry, and, when the sculpin came ashore, he seized it by its big, broad tail intending to eat it. But it slipped through his fingers. This happened many times, and each time the sculpin's tail became smaller. That is why it is so slender today. Then Raven said to it, "From now on you shall be named sculpin."

After this he went into the woods and set out to make the porcupine. For quills he took pieces of yellow cedar bark, which he set all the way up and down its back so that bears would be afraid of it. This is why bears never eat porcupines. He said to the porcupine, "Whenever anyone comes near you, throw your tail about." This is why people are afraid of it when it does so.

Now Raven went off to a certain place and made the west wind. He said to it, "You shall."

Raven also made the south wind. When the south wind climbs on top of a rock it never ceases to blow. He made the north wind, and on top of a mountain he made a house for it with something like ice hanging down on the sides. Then he went in and said to it, "Your sides are white." This is why the mountains are white with snow.

He also made the dog. It was at first a human being and did everything Raven wanted done, but he was too quick with everything, so Raven took him by the neck and pushed him down, saying, "You are nothing but a dog. You shall have four legs."

He made all the different races, as the Haida and the Tsimshian, the Tlingits' neighbors. They are human beings like the Tlingit, but he made their languages different.

Source: Adapted from "Raven," *Tlingit Myths and Texts.* John R. Swanton. Smithsonian Institution Bureau of American Ethnology Bulletin 39 (Washington, D.C.: Government Printing Office, 1909), pp. 3–21.

Coyote and Wolf Go to War with the Bushes

Coyote is by far the most widely-distributed and typical trickster in Native American folktales. In this narrative told by the Northern Paiute of the Great Basin area of the Western U.S., Coyote manifests his most common attributes: curiosity, impulsiveness leading to destructiveness, shape-shifting, and supernatural power. Wolf and Coyote are commonly paired, often as brothers, in Native American tales. As in the present instance, Wolf frequently suffers due to some character flaw of his trickster companion.

Wolf and Sagebrush were going to have a battle. Bullfrog was Wolf's partner. Greasewood and Sagebrush were partners. Bullfrog and Wolf had no bow and arrows. Wolf told Frog to get some sarvisberry sticks to make arrows. "Hurry up," he told Bullfrog.

That Wolf was the brother of Coyote. Coyote and Frog went after sarvisberry. They brought loads of it back for Wolf. That Wolf made arrows and put five at a time in one place. He talked to the arrows, and they finished themselves. The feathers went on by themselves when Wolf talked.

Sagebrush and the other Bushes had paint on their faces, and they came toward their enemies. Wolf put his brother, Coyote, inside the wickiup (dome-shaped dwelling) and shut him in tightly. They were going to have war with the Bushes, and only Wolf and Bullfrog were going to fight. When they started to fight, they yelled, "Ah ah ah ah ah ah ah."

When Wolf put his brother in the house, he shut it tight. "If there is a hole, tell me," he said to Coyote. But that Coyote did not tell him that there was one hole he could see through. "If you look outside, I might be killed," Wolf said to his brother.

The Bushes ran around that wickiup yelling, "Ya ya ya ya ya." Then that Coyote ran around inside the house.

He said, "Oh, I wish I could see how my brother is; he is making such a lot of noise." He jumped around. When he jumped, he saw Wolf through the hole.

Then that Wolf was killed. That Coyote did not believe his brother when he told him not to look out.

When Wolf was killed, Bullfrog went into a hole. The rough places on his skin are where he was shot. When he started into battle, he painted his back with white rock. He still has that mark on his back.

When those Bushes killed Wolf, they took his head. They cut off that head and took it with them. They were going to have a big time, those Bushes. They were going to have a big dance. They hung Wolf's head on a post. Coyote came out of the house, and he followed those people.

When his brother's head was on the post, he saw it. Those Bushes had a big fire, and they danced around. They had that head hanging in the middle of the circle.

One old woman who could hardly walk stayed home when everybody went to dance. That Coyote came to the old lady. He asked her, "Where are all the people? Why are you here alone?"

That old woman told Coyote, "The people have a head on a post, and they are going to dance tonight. Everybody is going to have a good time."

Coyote went where those people were gathered. He wanted to cry but he did not. He made himself into a strange person. He talked to those people, "Come on, everybody. I have a good song to sing." Then everybody came. They came when he said he was going to sing. Coyote sang, "Sleep tight all night, never wake up." His tail wagged as he danced. Then everybody danced so hard that they fell asleep right there.

Coyote grabbed his brother's head from the pole and ran. He stole Wolf's head from those people. The old woman who had stayed home saw Coyote take the head. She yelled, "Your head (trophy) is stolen," and everybody woke up. Then those Sagebrushes followed Coyote; they came chasing him. When they were close, that Coyote changed himself into a Sagebrush. They hunted and hunted for him, but they could not find him. Then they went home.

Coyote turned himself into Coyote again. He took his brother's head. He took water in his mouth, and he sprinkled it on that head. Then he buried the head in damp ground. Every night he did that, until finally the head turned into a person again.

Wolf called his brother. "Coyote," he said, "get up and make a fire." The next morning he was a man sitting by the fire.

Then Coyote said, "Oh, my brother, my brother." He grabbed him around the neck and hugged him; he was so glad to see his brother. He had made him into Wolf again. That's the way Coyote made his brother alive.

Source: Adapted from "Coyote and Wolf" in "Northern Paiute Tales," Isabel T. Kelly *Journal of American Folklore,* 51 (1938): 363–438, pp. 376–378.

How Coyote Joined the Dance of the Burrowing Owls

The following tale from Zuni Pueblo combines the qualities of both explanatory myth and cautionary tale. In many narratives, tricksters are portrayed as heroes who use their wits to overcome more powerful adversaries. In this instance, however, the trickster's negative traits of greed, idle curiosity, and gullibility prove destructive and serve as a warning to audience members against such antisocial behavior.

Y ou may know the country that lies south of the valley in which our town stands. You travel along the trail, which winds round the hill our ancients called the Hill of Grease, for the rocks sometimes shine in the light of the sun at evening, and it is said that strange things occurred there in the days of the ancients, which makes them thus to shine, while rocks of the kind in other places do not,—you travel on up this trail, crossing over the arroyos and foot-hills of the great mesa called Middle Mountain, until you come to the foot of the cliffs. Then you climb up back and forth, winding round and round, until you reach the top of the mountain, which is as flat as the floor of a house, merely being here and there traversed by small valleys covered with piñon and cedar, and threaded by trails made not only by the feet of our people but by deer and other animals. And so you go on and on, until, hardly knowing it, you have descended from the top of Middle Mountain, and found yourself in a wide plain covered with grass, and here and there clumps of trees. Beyond this valley is an elevated sandy plain, rather sunken in the middle, so that when it rains the water filters down into the soil of the depressed portion (which is wide enough to be a country in itself) and nourishes the grasses there; so that most of the year they grow green and sweet.

Now, a long, long time ago, in this valley or basin there lived a village of Prairie-dogs, on fairly peaceable terms with Rattlesnakes, Adders, Chameleons, Horned-toads, and Burrowing-owls. With the Owls they were especially friendly, looking at them as creatures of great gravity and sanctity. For this reason these Prairie-dogs and their companions never disturbed the councils or ceremonies of the Burrowing-owls, but treated them most respectfully, keeping at a distance from them when their dances were going on.

It chanced one day that the Burrowing-owls were having a great dance all to themselves, rather early in the morning. The dance they were engaged in was one peculiarly prized by them, requiring no little dexterity in its execution. Each dancer, young man or maiden, carried upon his or her head a bowl of foam, and though their legs were crooked and their motions disjointed, they danced to the whistling of some and the clapping beaks of others, in perfect unison, and with such dexterity that they never spilled a speck of the foam on their sleek mantles of dun-black feather-work.

It chanced this morning of the Foam-dance that a Coyote was nosing about for Grasshoppers and Prairie-dogs. So quite naturally he was prowling around the by-streets in the borders of the Prairie-dog town. His house where he lived with his old grandmother stood back to the westward, just over the elevations that bounded Sunken Country, among the rocks. He heard the click-clack of the musicians and their shrill, funny little song:

"I yami hota utchu tchapikya, Tokos! tokos! tokos! tokos!

So he pricked up his ears, and lifting his tail, trotted forward toward the level place between the hillocks and doorways of the village, where the Owls were dancing in a row. He looked at them with great curiosity, squatting on his haunches, the more composedly to observe them. Indeed, he became so much interested and amused by their shambling motions and clever evolutions, that he could no longer contain his curiosity. So he stepped forward, with a smirk and a nod toward the old master of ceremonies, and said: "My father, how are you and your children these many days?"

"Contented and happy," replied the old Owl, turning his attention to the dancing again.

"Yes, but I observe you are dancing," said the Coyote. "A very fine dance, upon my word! Charming! Charming! And why should you be dancing if you were not contented and happy, to be sure?"

"We are dancing," responded the Owl, "both for our pleasure and for the good of the town."

"True, true," replied the Coyote; "but what's that which looks like foam these dancers are carrying on their heads, and why do they dance in so limping a fashion?"

"You see, my friend," said the Owl, turning toward the Coyote, "we hold this to be a very sacred performance—very sacred indeed. Being such, these my children are initiated and so trained in the mysteries of the sacred society of which this is a custom that they can do very strange things in the observance of our ceremonies. You ask what it is that looks like foam they are balancing on their heads. Look more closely, friend. Do you not observe that it is their own grandmothers' heads they have on, the feathers turned white with age?"

"By my eyes!" exclaimed the Coyote, blinking and twitching his whiskers; "it seems so."

"And you ask also why they limp as they dance," said the Owl. "Now, this limp is essential to the proper performance of our dance—so essential, in fact, that in order to attain to it these my children go through the pain of having their legs broken. Instead of losing by this, they gain in a great many ways. Good luck always follows them. They are quite as spry as they were before, and enjoy, moreover, the distinction of performing a dance which no other people or creatures in the world are capable of!"

"Dust and devils!" ejaculated the Coyote. "This is passing strange. A most admirable dance, upon my word! Why, every bristle on my body keeps time to the music and their steps! Look here, my friend, don't you think that I could learn that dance?"

"Well," replied the old Owl; "it is rather hard to learn, and you haven't been initiated, you know; but, still, if you are determined that you would like to join the dance—by the way, have you a grandmother?"

"Yes, and a fine old woman she is," said he, twitching his mouth in the direction of his house. "She lives there with me. I dare say she is looking after my breakfast now."

"Very well," continued the old Owl, "if you care to join in our dance, fulfill the conditions, and I think we can receive you into our order." And he added, aside: "The silly fool; the sneaking, impertinent wretch! I will teach him to be sticking that sharp nose of his into other people's affairs!"

"All right! All right!" cried the Coyote, excitedly. "Will it last long?"

"Until the sun is so bright that it hurts our eyes," said the Owl; "a long time yet."

"All right! All right! I'll be back in a little while," said the Coyote; and, switching his tail into the air, away he ran toward his home. When he came to the house, he saw his old grandmother on the roof, which was a rock beside his hole, gathering fur from some skins, which he had brought home, to make up a bed for the Coyote's family.

"Ha, my blessed grandmother!" said the Coyote, "by means of your aid, what a fine thing I shall be able to do!"

The old woman was singing to herself when the Coyote dashed up to the roof where she was sitting, and, catching up a convenient leg-bone, whacked her over the pate and sawed her head off with the teeth of a deer. All bloody and soft as it was, he clapped it on his own head and raised himself on his hind-legs, bracing his tail against the ground, and letting his paws drop with the toes outspread, to imitate as nearly as possible the drooping wings of the dancing Owls. He found that it worked very well; so, descending with the head in one paw and a stone in the other, he found a convenient sharp-edged rock, and, laying his legs across it, hit them a tremendous crack with the stone, which broke them, to be sure, into splinters.

"Beloved Powers! Oh!" howled the Coyote. "Oh-o-o-o-o! the dance may be a fine thing, but the initiation is anything else!"

However, with his faith unabated, he shook himself together and got up to walk. But he could walk only with his paws; his hind-legs dragged helplessly behind him. Nevertheless, with great pain, and getting weaker and weaker every step of the way, he made what haste he could back to the Prairie-dog town, his poor old grandmother's head slung over his shoulders.

When he approached the dancers,—for they were still dancing,—they pretended to be greatly delighted with their new convert, and greeted him, notwithstanding his rueful countenance, with many congratulatory epithets, mingled with very proper and warm expressions of welcome. The Coyote looked sick and groaned occasionally and kept looking around at his feet, as though he would like to lick them. But the old Owl extended his wing and cautioned him not to interfere with the working power of faith in this essential observance, and invited him (with an "Ahem!" that very much resembled a suppressed giggle), to join in their dance. The Coyote smirked and bowed and tried to stand up gracefully on his stumps, but fell over, his grandmother's head rolling around in the dirt. He picked up the grisly head, clapped it on his crown again and raised himself, and with many a howl, which he tried in vain to check, began to prance around; but ere long tumbled over again. The Burrowing-owls were filled with such merriment at his discomfiture that they laughed until they spilled the foam all down their backs and bosoms; and, with a parting fling at the Coyote, which gave him to understand that he had made a fine fool of himself, and would know better than to pry into other people's business next time, skipped away to a safe distance from him.

Then, seeing how he had been tricked, the Coyote fell to howling and clapping his thighs; and, catching sight of his poor grandmother's head, all bloody and begrimed with dirt, he cried out in grief and anger: "Alas! alas! that it should have come to this! You little devils! I'll be even with you! I'll smoke you out of your holes."

"What will you smoke us out with?" tauntingly asked the Burrowing-owls.

"Ha! You'll find out. With yucca!"

"O! O! ha! ha!" laughed the Owls. "That is our succotash!"

"Ah, well! I'll smoke you out!" yelled the Coyote, stung by their taunts.

"What with?" cried the Owls.

"Grease-weed."

"He, ha! ho, ho! We make our mush-stew of that!"

"Ha! but I'll smoke you out, nevertheless, you little beasts!"

"What with? What with?" shouted the Owls.

"Yellow-top weeds," said he.

"Ha, ha! All right; smoke away! We make our sweet gruel with that, you fool!"

"I'll fix you! I'll smoke you out! I'll suffocate the very last one of you!"

"What with? What with?" shouted the Owls, skipping around on their crooked feet.

"Pitch-pine," snarled the Coyote.

This frightened the Owls, for pitch-pine, even to this day, is sickening to them. Away they plunged into their holes, pell-mell.

Then the Coyote looked at his poor old grandmother's begrimed and bloody head, and cried out—just as Coyotes do now at sunset, I suppose— "Oh, my poor, poor grandmother! So this is what they have caused me to do to you!" And, tormented both by his grief and his pain, he took up the head of his grandmother and crawled back as best he could to his house.

When he arrived there he managed to climb up to the roof, where her body lay stiff. He chafed her legs and sides, and washed the blood and dirt from her head, and got a bit of sinew, and sewed her head to her body as carefully as he could and as hastily. Then he opened her mouth, and, putting his muzzle to it, blew into her throat, in the hope of resuscitating her; but the wind only leaked out from the holes in her neck, and she gave no signs of animation. Then the Coyote mixed some pap of fine toasted meal and water and poured it down her throat, addressing her with vehement expressions of regret at what he had done, and apology and solicitation that she should not mind, as he did not mean it, and imploring her to revive. But the pap only trickled out between the stitches in her neck, and she grew colder and stiffer all the while; so that at last the Coyote gave it up, and, moaning, he betook himself to a near clump of piñon trees, intent upon vengeance and designing to gather pitch with which to smoke the Owls to death. But, weakened by his injuries, and filled with grief and shame and mortification, when he got there he could only lie down.

He was so engrossed in howling and thinking of his woes and pains that a Horned-toad, who saw him, and who hated him because of the insults he had frequently suffered from him and his kind, crawled into the throat of the beast without his noticing it. Presently, the little creature struck up a song.

"Ah-a-a-a-a-a," the Coyote was groaning. But—when he heard this song, apparently far off, and yet so near, he felt very strangely inside, so he thought and no doubt wondered if it were the song of some musician. At any rate, he lifted his head and looked all around, but hearing nothing, lay down again and bemoaned his fate.

Then the Horned-toad sang again. This time the Coyote called out immediately, and the Horned-toad answered, "Here I am."

But look as he would, the Coyote could not find the Toad. So he listened for the song again, and heard it, and asked who it was that was singing. The Horned-toad replied that it was he. But still the Coyote could not find him. A fourth time the Horned-toad sang, and the Coyote began to suspect that it was under him. So he lifted himself to see; and one of the spines on the Horned-toad's neck pricked him, and at the same time the little fellow called out: "Here I am, you idiot, inside of you! I came upon you here, and being a medicine-man of some prominence, I thought I would explore your vitals and see what was the matter."

"By the souls of my ancestors!" exclaimed the Coyote, "be careful what you do in there!"

The Horned-toad replied by laying his hand on the Coyote's liver, and exclaiming: "What is this I feel?"

"Where?" said the Coyote.

"Down here."

"Merciful daylight! It is my liver, without which no one can have solidity of any kind, or a proper vitality. Be very careful not to injure that; if you do, I shall die at once, and what will become of my poor wife and children?"

Then the Horned-toad climbed up to the stomach of the Coyote. "What is this, my friend?" said he, feeling the sides of the Coyote's food-bag.

"What is it like?" asked the Coyote.

"Wrinkled," said the Horned-toad, "and filled with a fearful mess of stuff!"

"Oh! mercy! mercy! Good daylight! My precious friend, be very careful! That is the very source of my being—my stomach itself!"

"Very well," said the Horned-toad. Then he moved on somewhat farther and touched the heart of the Coyote, which startled him fearfully. "What is this?" cried the Horned-toad.

"Mercy, mercy! What are you doing?" exclaimed the Coyote.

"Nothing—feeling of your vitals," was the reply. "What is it?"

"Oh, what is it like?" said the Coyote.

"Shaped like a pine-nut, "said the Horned-toad, "as nearly as I can make out; it keeps leaping so."

"Leaping, is it?" howled the Coyote. "Mercy! my friend, get away from there! That is the very heart of my being, the thread that ties my existence, the home of my emotions, and my knowledge of daylight. Go away from there, do, I pray you! If you should scratch it ever so little, it would be the death of me, and what would my wife and children do?"

"Hey!" said the Horned-toad, "you wouldn't be apt to insult me and my people any more if I touched you up there a little, would you?" And he hooked one of his horns into the Coyote's heart. The Coyote gave one gasp, straightened out his limbs, and expired.

"Ha, ha! you villain! Thus would you have done to me, had you found the chance; thus unto you"—saying which he found his way out and sought the nearest water-pocket he could find.

So you see from this, which took place in the days of the ancients, it may be inferred that the instinct of meddling with everything that did not concern him, and making a universal nuisance of himself, and desiring to imitate everything that he sees, ready to jump into any trap that is laid for him, is a confirmed instinct with the Coyote, for those are precisely his characteristics today.

Furthermore, Coyotes never insult Horned-toads nowadays, and they keep clear of Burrowing-owls. And ever since then the Burrowing-owls have been speckled with gray and white all over their backs and bosoms, because their ancestors spilled foam over themselves in laughing at the silliness of the Coyote.

Source: "How Coyote Joined the Dance of the Burrowing Owls" from Zuni Folktales by Frank Hamilton Cushing (New York: G.P. Putnam's Sons. 1901) pp. 203–215.

Manabozho's Adventures

Unlike the animal tricksters, Raven and Coyote, encountered in the tales of the Northwest Coast, the Southwest, and the Great Basin, the Menomini and many of the other Native American cultures of the Great Lakes and Northeastern Woodlands embraced a human trickster known as Manabozho (or some variant of this name). Despite his form, Manabozho displays all the contradictions of his counterparts from the animal world: cleverness and foolishness, guile and gullibility. Like Coyote and Raven he wanders aimlessly from adventure to misadventure, shaping elements of the natural and social environment in the manner of a haphazard culture hero. (Compare his exploits to Raven's in Raven Befriends Human Race*).*

Manabozho saw a number of ducks, and he thought to himself, "Just how am I going to kill them?" After a while, he took out one of his pails and started to drum and sing at the same time. The words of the song he sang were:

"I am bringing new songs."

When the ducks saw Manabozho standing near the shore, they swam toward him and as soon as he saw this, he sent his grandmother ahead to build a little lodge, where they could live. In the meantime, he killed a few of the ducks, so, while his grandmother started out to build a shelter, Manabozho went toward the lake where the ducks and geese were floating round and round. Manabozho jumped into a sack and then dived into the water.

The ducks and geese were quite surprised to see that he was such an excellent diver, and came closer and closer. Then Manabozho challenged them to a contest at diving. He said that he could beat them all. The ducks all accepted the challenge, but Manabozho beat them. Then he went after the geese and beat them too.

For a time he was alternately diving and rising to the surface, all around. Finally, he dived under the geese and started to tie their legs together with some basswood bark. When the geese noticed this, they tried to rise and fly away, but they were unable to do so, for Manabozho was hanging on to the other end of the string.

The geese, nevertheless, managed to rise, gradually dragging Manabozho along with them. They finally emerged from the water and rose higher and higher into the air. Manabozho, however, hung on, and would not let go, until his hand was cut and the string broke.

While walking along the river he saw some berries in the water. He dived down for them, but was stunned when he unexpectedly struck the bottom. There he lay for quite a while, and when he recovered consciousness and looked up, he saw the berries hanging on a tree just above him.

While Manabozho was once walking along a lake shore, tired and hungry, he observed a long, narrow sandbar, which extended far out into the water, around which were myriads of waterfowl, so Manabozho decided to have a feast. He had with him only his medicine bag; so he entered the brush and hung it upon a tree, now called "Manabozho tree," and procured a quantity of bark, which he rolled into a bundle and placing it upon his back, returned to the shore, where he pretended to pass slowly by, in sight of the birds. Some of the Swans and Ducks, however, recognizing Manabozho and becoming frightened, moved away from the shore.

One of the Swans called out, "Ho! Manabozho, where are you going?"

To this Manabozho replied, "I am going to have a song. As you may see, I have all my songs with me." Manabozho then called out to the birds, "Come to me, my brothers, and let us sing and dance." The birds assented and returned to the shore, when all retreated a short distance away from the lake to an open space where they might dance. Manabozho removed the bundle of bark from his back and placed it on the ground and said to the birds, "Now, all of you dance around me as I drum; sing as loudly as you can, and keep your eyes closed. The first one to open his eyes will forever have them red and sore."

Manabozho began to beat time upon his bundle of bark, while the birds, with eyes closed, circled around him singing as loudly as they could. Keeping time with one hand, Manabozho suddenly grasped the neck of a Swan, which he broke; but before he had killed the bird it screamed out, whereupon Manabozho said, "That's right, brothers, sing as loudly as you can." Soon another Swan fell a victim; then a Goose, and so on until the number of birds was greatly reduced.

Then the "Hell-diver," opening his eyes to see why there was less singing than at first, and beholding Manabozho and the heap of victims, cried out, "Manabozho is killing us! Manabozho is killing us!" and immediately ran to the water, followed by the remainder of the birds.

As the "Hell-diver" was a poor runner, Manabozho soon overtook him, and said, "I won't kill you, but you shall always have red eyes and be the laughing stock of all the birds." With this he gave the bird a kick, sending him far out into the lake and knocking off his tail, so that the "Hell-diver" is red-eyed and tailless to this day.

Manabozho then gathered up his birds, and taking them out upon the sandbar buried them—some with their heads protruding, others with the feet sticking out of the sand. He then built a fire to cook the game, but as this would require some time, and as Manabozho was tired after his exertion, he stretched himself on the ground to sleep. In order to be informed if anyone approached, he slapped his thigh and said to it, "You watch the birds, and awaken me if anyone should come near them." Then, with his back to the fire, he fell asleep.

After awhile a party of Indians came along in their canoes, and seeing the feast in store, went to the sandbar and pulled out every bird, which Manabozho had so carefully placed there, but put back the heads and feet in such a way that there was no indication that the bodies had been disturbed. When the Indians had finished eating they departed, taking with them all the food that remained from the feast.

Some time afterward, Manabozho awoke, and, being very hungry, bethought himself to enjoy the fruits of his stratagem. In attempting to pull a baked swan from the sand he found nothing but the head and neck, which he held in his hand. Then he tried another, and found the body of that bird also gone. So he tried another, and then another, but each time met with disappointment. Who could have robbed him? he thought. He struck his thigh and asked, "Who has been here to rob me of my feast; did I not command you to watch while I slept?"

His thigh responded, "I also fell asleep, as I was very tired; but I see some people moving rapidly away in their canoes; perhaps they were the thieves. I see also they are very dirty and poorly dressed." Then Manabozho ran out to the point of the sandbar, and beheld the people in their canoes, just disappearing around a point of land. Then he called to them and reviled them, calling them "Winnibe'go! Winnibe'go!" (Winnebago, "People of the Stinking Water"). And by this term the Menomini have ever since designated their thievish neighbors.

After this Manabozho began traveling again. One time he feasted a lot of animals. He had killed a big bear, which was very fat and he began cooking it, having made a fire with his bow-drill. When he was ready to spread his meat, he heard two trees scraping together, swayed by the wind. He did not like this noise while he was having his feast and he thought he could stop it. He climbed up one of the trees and when he reached the spot where the two trees were scraping, his foot got caught in a crack between the trees and he could not free himself.

When the first animal guest came along and saw Manabozho in the tree, he, the Beaver, said "Come on to the feast, Manabozho is caught and can't stop us." And then the other animals came. The Beaver jumped into the grease and ate it, and the Otter did the same, and that is why they are so fat in the belly. The Beaver scooped up the grease and smeared it on himself, and that is the reason why he is so fat now. All the small animals came and got fat for themselves. Last of all the animals came the Rabbit, when nearly all the grease was gone—only a little left. So he put some on the nape of his neck and some on his groin and for this reason he has only a little fat in those places. So all the animals got their fat except Rabbit.

Then they all went, and poor Manabozho got free at last. He looked around and found a bear's skull that was all cleaned except for the brain, and there was only a little of that left, but he could not get at it. Then he wished himself to be changed into an ant in order to get into the skull and get enough to eat, for there was only about an ant's meal left.

Then he became an ant and entered the skull. When he had enough he turned back into a man, but he had his head inside the skull; this allowed him to walk but not to see. On account of this he had no idea where he was. Then he felt the trees. He said to one, "What are you?"

It answered, "Cedar." He kept doing this with all the trees in order to keep his course. When he got too near the shore, he knew it by the kind of trees he met. So he kept on walking and the only tree that did not answer promptly was the black spruce, and that said "I'm Black Spruce. Then Manabozho knew he was on low ground.

He came to a lake, but he did not know how large it was, as he could not see. He started to swim across. An Ojibwa was paddling on the lake with his family and he heard someone calling, "Hey! There's a bear swimming across the lake." Manabozho became frightened at this and the Ojibwa then said, "He's getting near the shore now." So Manabozho swam faster, and as he could understand the Ojibwa language, he guided himself by the cries. He landed on a smooth rock, slipped and broke the bear's skull, which fell off his head. Then the Ojibwa cried out, "That's no bear! That's Manabozho!" Manabozho was all right, now that he could see, so he ran off, as he did not want to stay with these people.

Source: Adapted from "Manabozho" from *Tales of the North American Indians,* Stith Thompson (Bloomington: Indiana University Press, 1929), pp. 53–57.

SOCIETY AND CONFLICT

The Punishment of the Stingy

In the traditional narratives of the Chinook of Oregon, Blue jay was a stock character who represented the "anti-citizen." His role was to violate all social norms and by doing so to reinforce proper behavior. His violation in the following tale is especially serious; in societies that base their survival on hunting and gathering their food supply, greed is a gravely antisocial act. Withholding food from one's own family members is unthinkable. Thus, the drastic punishment of Blue jay and his followers is consistent with Chinook social codes.

At Sea Side lived many people—a big village. Their houses were on the bank, and, below, the wide beach sloped down to the salt water. Under the bank the canoes rested on the beach above high-water mark. Beyond was the sea.

One day the Chief of the village died. He had one son, a big boy just growing up to be a man. It was winter, and the people had hardly anything to eat. They looked along the beach for food cast up by the sea, but they could find nothing. They were hungry, and did not know what they should do. Mussels and roots were their only food.

One day a hunter said to the men: "Everybody get ready; let us go out to sea. Perhaps there we may find something to eat; even if we kill nothing, we can at least gather mussels."

So all the men got ready, and they started out to sea in two canoes. After they had gone some distance they came to a small island, and saw there some sea-lions, and the hunter speared one, and it jumped out to the water and swam strongly, and then it died and floated on the water.

They dragged it up on the shore near by, and Blue jay said, "We will boil it here." So they made a fire there and singed it, cut it up, and boiled it. Then Blue jay said: "Let us eat it here. Let us eat all of it, and not take any of it home with us." So these people ate there.

The Raven wished to take home some of the meat to give to persons who were hungry, and hid a piece in his mat and carried it to the canoe, but Blue jay ran down and took the meat and threw it into the fire and burned it. After they had eaten all they wanted, they made ready to go home. They gathered mussels, large and small.

In the evening they came to the village, and Blue jay called out to his wife, "Come and get your mussels." There was a noise of many feet as Blue jay's wife and the other women came running down to get their mussels, and carried them up to the houses.

The Raven took care of the Chief's son. That night the boy said to him, "Tomorrow I want to go with you."

Blue jay said: "What are you going to do? The waves will carry you away. You will be washed away. I was almost washed away."

Early the next morning the men made ready to go hunting again. They went down to the beach and got into the canoes, and the boy also went down to the beach. He intended to go with them, and as they were pushing off he tried to get into one of the canoes. Blue jay said to him, "Go up to the houses. Go up to the houses."

The boy went, as he had been told, but he felt very sorry, and then Blue jay said, "Quick, let us leave him." The people began to paddle.

At length they reached the land where they had been the day before. It was a rocky island. The hunter went ashore and speared a sea-lion. They hauled it to the shore and pulled it up on land, and then pulled it up away from the beach. Blue jay said, "We will eat it all here, or else our Chief's son will always be wanting to come with us." So now they singed the sea-lion, and cut it up and boiled it there. Then, when what they were cooking was ready, they ate plenty. The Raven tried to save one piece of the meat. He tied it in his hair, intending to hide it, but Blue jay took it out and threw it into the fire and burned it.

When they started home they gathered mussels, and at evening they got home. Before they landed, Blue jay called out loud, "Come, my wife, and get your mussels." There was a noise of feet running, and Blue jay's wife and her children came running to the beach with all the other women. Then they carried the mussels up to the houses. Blue jay said to the men who had been with him, "Do not tell the Chief's son, any of you, for if you do he will always go with us."

That night the boy said, "Tomorrow I am going with you"; and Blue jay said to him: "What are you going to do? You may drift away. You may be overwhelmed by the waves."

The boy said, "I will go with you."

On the third morning they rose early and went to the beach, and the boy also went to the beach, and took hold of the side of the canoe to get in. Blue jay said, "What are you doing here? Go to the houses." The boy cried, but he went back. Then Blue jay said to the others, "Quick, paddle; we will leave him behind." Then the people paddled away.

At length they arrived at the rock of the sea-lions, and the hunter went ashore. He speared a large sea-lion, and pretty soon it floated dead on the water. They pulled it in to the shore and up on the beach, and then they hauled it up above the beach and singed and cut it up and boiled it there. When it was done they ate, and Blue jay said: "We will eat it all. We will

not tell any one, for fear that our Chief's son should want to come with us."
After all had eaten enough, a little meat was still left. The Raven tried to hide
a piece of it. He tied it to his leg and put a bandage over it, and said that his
leg was broken. Blue jay burned all the meat that was left over. He said to
the Raven, "I want to see your leg." He seized the Raven's leg and untied
it, and found the piece of meat that the Raven had tied to it and burned it.
Towards evening they gathered mussels, and then they went home.

When they were nearly at their home Blue jay called out, "My wife, your
mussels." There was a noise of feet, and Blue jay's and the women ran to the
beach. They carried the mussels up from the beach and ate mussels all night.

The boy said, "Tomorrow, I think, I shall surely go along with you."

Blue jay said to him: "What are you going to do? You will drift away.
I should have drifted away twice if I had not caught hold of the canoe."

Early the next morning they made themselves ready, and the boy got up
and made himself ready. Then the people hauled their canoes down to the
water and got into them. The boy tried to get into a canoe too, but Blue-
jay took hold of him and threw him into the water. He stood in the water
up to his waist. He took hold of the side of the canoe, but Blue-jay hit his
hands to make him let go. For a long time he held on, and cried and cried,
but at last he let go and went up to the house.

Then Blue jay and the other people paddled away. After a while they
reached the rock where the sea-lions lived, and the hunter went ashore and
speared a sea-lion, and it jumped into the water and soon floated there dead.
Then they towed it to the beach and pulled it up and singed it, and cut it up
and boiled it. Blue jay said, "We will eat it here." They ate for a long time
and ate half of it, and then they were satisfied. They were so full that they
went to sleep. After a while Blue jay awoke and burned all the meat that
was left. Toward evening they gathered mussels and then started home.

When they were near the shore, Blue jay called out to his wife, "Come and
get your mussels, my wife," and they heard the noise of feet running down to
the shore. Then they carried up the mussels from the beach. That night the
boy said, "Tomorrow I shall go with you"; and Blue jay said to him: "What
are you going to do? We may be thrown into the water and you may drown."

Early the next morning the men made ready to start. The boy also got up
and made himself ready. Then Blue jay and the people hauled the canoes
down to the water and got into them. The boy tried to get into the canoe,
but Blue-jay threw him into the water, and they pushed off. The boy caught
hold of the side of the canoe and held it. He stood there in the water up to his
armpits, and tried to get into the canoe, but Blue jay hit his hands and made
him let go. The boy cried and cried. Blue jay and the hunters paddled away.

After a little time the boy went up to the beach, feeling very sad, and trying to think what he should do. At last he went into the house and took his
arrows and started walking along the shore. He walked around a point, and
saw a black eagle, and shot it. He skinned it and tried to put the skin

on his body, but it was too small. It did not reach down as far as his knees. He took it off and left it there and went on.

After a while he saw another eagle, and he shot it, and it fell down. Its head was partly white. He skinned it and put the skin on his body, but it was too small. It reached down only a little below his knees. Then he took it off and left it lying there, and went on a long way. At last he saw a bald-headed eagle. He shot it, and it fell down. Then he skinned it and put the skin on himself. Even this was too small, but it nearly fitted him. Then he tried to fly. At first he could only fly downward. He could not rise in the air. He tried again, and this time he found that he could turn, so he kept on trying, and pretty soon he could fly well.

Now he flew toward the village, and when he had come near to this point he smelled smoke, and in that smoke he smelled fat cooking. So before he got to the village he turned and flew out to sea, following the smell of the smoke. Pretty soon he came to the rock of the sea lions, and there he saw the men of his village. He lit on a tree far off and watched them, looking down on them below. He saw that they were cooking, and when the meat was done he saw them eating. When they had nearly finished eating, he flew towards them, and he thought, "I wish Blue jay would see me."

Blue jay did see the bird flying, and he said, "Ha! A bird is coming to get food from us." The boy flew around them once, and then again. Five times he circled around them, all the time coming lower. Blue jay took a piece of meat and threw it out, and said to the bird, "I give you this to eat; take it." The bird came down, and, grasping the piece of meat, flew away. Then Blue jay said, "Why, that bird has feet just like a person!"

When Blue jay and the people had finished eating they went to sleep. Again the Raven hid a piece of meat. Toward evening Blue jay awoke, and then the people ate again, and afterwards Blue jay burned what they had left. Then they gathered mussels and started to go home.

When they were close to the houses Blue jay called out, "Ah, my wife, get your mussels." All the women ran down to the beach with a noise of feet, and carried up the mussels.

When the boy got home he at once lay down. That evening the people tried to wake him, but he did not rise.

The next morning, as soon as it became day, early, they began to get ready, and again they hauled their canoes into the water. The Chief's son still lay in bed. He did not try to go with them, and they started off.

After a while the sun rose. Then the boy got up. He called together all the women and children and said to them: "Quick, wash yourselves. Hurry; don't be lazy." They all washed themselves. Then he said, "Quick, comb your hair." They did so.

Then he put down a plank on the ground and took a piece of meat from under his blanket, and said to them, "All your husbands eat a great deal of this meat every day." He put two pieces of the meat side by side on the plank. Then he cut off a piece of the meat and greased the heads of all the women and the children. Then he pulled out of the ground the wall planks of the houses and sharpened them. If a wall plank was wide, he split it. He sharpened all of them. The Raven's house was the last house in the village. He did not pull down its planks. He fastened the planks on the backs of the women, and said to the women, "Now go to the beach and swim towards the sea, and as you go, swim five times around that rock and then go out to sea. After this you shall be killer whales. When you find sea-lions you shall always kill them, but do not give any of them to stingy people. When you kill a good whale you shall eat it, but do not give any of it to stingy people. I shall take these children with me. They shall live on the sea and be my relations." Then he began to split sinews; he split a great many of them. He threw down the sinews that he had split on the stones where the people used to gather their mussels, and said to the mussels, "After this when Blue jay and these others go to take up you mussels, you shall always be tied fast to the rocks."

Now the women went down to the water's edge and swam about, and began slowly to jump out of the water. Five times they swam backward and forward before the village; then they went seaward, swimming very fast. They kept on to the island where Blue jay and his fellows were cooking their food. Blue jay said to the men, "What is this that is coming?" The men looked at the things that were coming, and saw the women often jumping out of the water. Five times they swam around that rock, then they went out to sea. After a while birds came flying after them toward the sea—birds with red bills, just as if blood were on their beaks. They kept following one another, many of them. Blue jay said: "Do you see these birds, how they keep coming? Where do they come from?"

Then the Raven said, "How is it that you do not recognize these as your children?" Five times the birds flew around the rock, just as the women had gone around it, and then they flew away out to sea.

When Blue jay and his people were eating the meat that they had killed, that hunter said: "Quick, let us go home. I am afraid that we have seen bad spirits. We never before saw anything like this at this rock." Then they gathered some mussels, and put in the canoes the meat that was left and carried it with them.

Just at evening they came to the village, and Blue jay called out, "Ah, Wife, come and get your mussels." There was no noise of people running. Five times he called to her, but no one came. It was all still. They went up on the beach, and then they saw that no one was there, and that the walls of the houses had disappeared. Then they began to cry, and Blue-jay cried too.

Some one said to him, "Be quiet, Blue jay; if you had not been bad, our Chief would not have done this to us."

Now they made only one house for all; all lived together. Only the Raven, who had been kindhearted, had a house to himself. He often went along the beach looking for food, and was lucky, for sometimes he found a sturgeon, or again he went along the beach looking for food and he found a porpoise. Blue jay often went along the beach trying to find food, but he was always unlucky, for he found nothing, and often, while he was looking, suddenly it would begin to hail—big hailstones. Often he went out to gather mussels and tried to break them off from the rocks, but he could not do it. They were stuck fast to the stones. So he gave up and went home. He cried a great deal. Often the Raven looked for food along the beach and found a seal. The others had nothing to eat except roots.

Thus these men who had not brought food to their families had now lost their women and children, their houses had been pulled down and taken away, and they had nothing to eat. So their Chief punished them for being stingy.

Source: Adapted from "The Punishment of the Stingy." *The Punishment of the Stingy and Other Indian Stories,* George Bird Grinnell (New York: Harper & Brother Publishers, 1901), pp. 3–15.

Kasiagsak, the Great Liar

The traditional subsistence of the arctic Inuit (Eskimo) was based to a great extent on protein obtained from the maritime mammals mentioned in the following narrative. Failure in the hunt, whether from lack of skill or lack of initiative, resulted in a virtual death sentence for one's family unit. Moreover, in the harsh arctic environment with its scant resources, Kasiagsak's efforts at surviving by exploiting his neighbors endangered not only his own kin, but all those linked to it. Therefore, the justice meted out according to Inuit custom was a logical consequence of his antisocial behavior.

Kasiagsak, who was living with a great many skillful seal-hunters, always returned in the evening without a catch of his own. When he was out, his wife, named Kitlagsuak, was always restless and fidgety, running out and in looking out for him, in the hope that he might be bringing home something; but he generally returned empty-handed.

One day, being out in his kayak, he observed a black spot on a piece of ice, and it soon turned to be a little seal. His first intention was to harpoon it, but he changed his mind, and broke out, saying, "Poor little thing! It is almost a pity. Perhaps it has already been wounded by somebody else; perhaps it will slide down in the water when I approach it, and then I need only take hold of it with my hands." So saying he gave a shout, at which the seal was not slow to get down. Presently, it appeared close before the point of his kayak; but he called out still louder than before, and the seal went on diving up and down quite close to him. At length he made up his mind to chase and harpoon it; but somehow it always rose at a greater distance, and was soon entirely lost to him. Kasiagsak now put back, merely observing, "You silly thing! You are not easy to get at, but just wait till next time."

Another day he went seaward in bright, fine weather. Looking toward land he got sight of the other kayakers, and observed that one of them had just harpooned a seal, and that the others were all hurrying on to his assistance. As to himself, he never stirred, but remained quite unconcerned in his former place. He also noticed that the one who had caught the seal tugged it to the shore, and made it fast to a rock on the beach, intending to

return in pursuit of others. He instantly put further out to sea; but when he
had got quite out of sight he returned to the beach by a roundabout way,
and made straight for the other man's seal, and carried it off. The towing-
line was all around ornamented with walrus-teeth, and he was greatly
delighted at the prospect of getting home with this prize.

Meanwhile his wife had been wandering about in expectation of him and
looking out for the returning kayakers. She at length cried out, "There is a
kayak!" at which more people came running out; and shading her eyes with
her hand, she continued, "It looks like Kasiagsak, and he moves his arms
like one tugging something along with him. Well, I suppose it will now be
my turn to give you a share, and you shall all get a nice piece of blubber."

As soon as he landed she hastened to ask him, "Where did you get that
beautiful tugging-line?"

He answered, "This morning at setting out I thought it might come in
handy, as I was bent on having a catch, and so I brought it out with me;
I have kept it in store this long time." "Have you, indeed?" she rejoined,
and then began the skinning and carving business. She put the head, the
back, and the skin aside; all the rest, as well as the blubber, she intended to
make a grand feast upon. The other kayakers successively returned, and
she took care to inform each of them separately that a seal was already
brought home; and when some of the women came back from a ramble on
the beach, she repeated the whole thing over to them.

But while they were sitting down to supper in the evening, a boy entered,
saying, "I have been sent to ask for the towing-line; as to the seal, that is no
matter."

Turning to Kasiagsak, his wife now put in, "Did you tell me an untruth?"

He only answered, "To be sure I did," whereto his wife remarked, "What
a shame it is that Kasiagsak behaves thus!" but he only made a wry face,
saying, "Bah!" which made her quite frightened; and when they lay down
to rest he went on pinching her and whistling until they both fell asleep.

Another day, rowing about in his kayak, he happened to observe a black
spot away on a flake of ice. On nearing it he made it out to be only a stone.
He glanced around toward the other kayakers, and then suddenly feigned to
be rowing hard up to a seal, at the same time lifting the harpoon ready to
lance it; but presently went to hide himself behind a projecting point of the
ice, from which he managed to climb it and roll the stone into the sea with
a splash, making it all froth and foam. Meanwhile he got into his kayak
again, making a great roar in order to call the others to his assistance. When
they came up to him they observed that he had no bladder [used as a float for
his harpoon and line], and he said, "A walrus has just gone down with my
bladder; do help me to catch sight of him; meantime I will turn back and tell
the others at home that I have lanced a walrus."

He hurried landward, and his wife, who happened to be on the lookout,
again shouted, "A kayaker!"

He called out that he had made a lucky hit. "I almost do believe it is Kasiagsak; do ye hear him in there?"

Meantime he had approached the shore, and said, "In chasing a walrus I lost my bladder; I only came home to tell you this."

His wife now came running into the house, but being in such a hurry she broke the handle of her knife. However, she did not mind this, but merely said, "Now I can get a handle of walrus-tooth for my knife, and a new hook for my kettle." In the evening Kasiagsak had chosen a seat on the hindermost part of the ledge, so that only his heels were to be seen. The other kayakers stayed out rather long; but the last of them on entering brought a harpoon-line and a bladder along with him, and turning to Kasiagsak observed, "I think it is yours; it must have been tied round some stone and have slipped off; here it is."

His wife exclaimed, "Have you been telling us new lies?" at which he only answered her, "Why, yes; I wanted to play you a trick, you see."

Another day, when he was kayaking along the coast, he saw some loose pieces of ice away on a sandy beach at some distance; he rowed up to them and went ashore. Two women, gathering berries, watched his doings all along. They saw him fill his kayak with bits of broken ice; and this done, he waded down into the water till it reached his very neck, and then turned back and got upon the beach, where he set to hammering his kayak all over with stones; and having finally stuffed his coat with ice, he turned towards home.

At some distance he commenced shrieking aloud and crying, "Ah me! A big iceberg went calving (bursting and capsizing) right across my kayak, and came down on the top of me"; and his wife repeated his ejaculations, adding, "I must go and see about some dry clothes for him."

At last they got him up on shore, and large bits of ice came tumbling out of his clothes, while he went on lamenting and groaning as if with pain, saying, "I had a very narrow escape." His wife repeated the tale of his misfortunes to every kayaker on his return home; but at last it so happened that the two women who had seen him likewise returned, and they at once exclaimed, "Is not that he whom we saw down below the sand-cliffs, stuffing his clothes with ice."

On this, the wife cried out, "Dear me! has Kasiagsak again been lying to us?" Subsequently Kasiagsak went to pay a visit to his father-in-law. On entering the house he exclaimed, "Why, what's the matter with you that your lamps are not burning, and ye are boiling dog's flesh?"

"Alas!" answered the master, pointing to his little son, "he was hungry, poor fellow, and having nothing else to eat we killed the dog."

Kasiagsak boastingly answered him, "Yesterday we had a hard job at home. One of the women and I had our hands full with the great heaps of seals and walruses that have been caught. I have got both my storehouses choke-full with them; my arms are quite sore with the work." The father-in-law now rejoined, "Who would ever have thought that the poor little

orphan boy Kasiagsak should turn out such a rich man!" and so saying, he
began crying with emotion, and Kasiagsak feigned crying likewise.

On parting from them the following day, he proposed that his little
brother-in-law should accompany him in order to bring back some victuals,
adding, "I will see you home again," and his father said, "Well, don't you
hear what thy brother-in-law is saying? You had better go."

On reaching home, Kasiagsak took hold of a string and brought it into the
house, where he busied himself in making a trap, and taking some scraps of
frizzled blubber from his wife's lamp, he thrust them out as baits for the rav-
ens. Suddenly be gave a pull at the string, crying out, "Two! Alas! One made
its escape"; and then be ran out and brought back a raven, which his wife
skinned and boiled. But his brother-in-law had to look to the other people
for some food; and at his departure the next day, he likewise received all
his presents from them, and not from Kasiagsak.

Another day Kasiagsak set off in his kayak to visit some people at a neigh-
boring station. Having entered one of the houses, he soon noticed that some
of the inmates were mourning the loss of some one deceased. He questioned
the others, and on hearing that they had lost a little daughter named Nepisanguak, he hastened in a loud voice to state, "We have just got a little
daughter at home, whom we have called Nepisanguak"; on which the
mourning parents and relations exclaimed, "Thanks be to you that you have
called her by that name"; and then they wept, and Kasiagsak also made
believe to be weeping; but he peeped through his fingers all the while. Later
in the day they treated him richly with plenty of good things to eat. Kasiagsak went on saying, "Our little daughter cannot speak plainly as yet; she
only cries 'bees!'" but the others said, "She surely means 'beads,' we will
give you some for her"; and at his departure he was loaded with gifts such
as beads, a plate, and some seal meat.

Just as he was going to start, one of the men cried out to him, "I would
like to buy a kayak, and I can pay it back with a good pot; make it known
to the people in your place." But Kasiagsak said, "Give it to me; I have got
a new kayak, but it is a little too narrow for my size." At length be started
along with his presents, and the pot stuck upon the front part of his kayak.

At home be said, "Such a dreadful accident! A boat must surely have been
lost; all these things I bring you here, I have found tossed about on the ice";
and his wife hastened into the house to give her cracked old pot a smash, and
threw away the shoulder-blades that till now had served her instead of
plates, and ornamented her coat with beads, and proudly walked to and
fro to make the pearls rattle.

The next day a great many kayakers were announced. Kasiagsak instantly
kept as far back on the ledge as possible. As soon as the kayakers put in to
shore, they called out, "Tell Kasiagsak to come down and fetch off some
victuals we have brought for their little daughter"; but all the reply was,
"Why, they have got no daughter at all."

Another of the men now put in, "Go and ask Kasiagsak for the new kayak I bought of him"; but the answer was, "He certainly has no new kayak." At this information they quickly got up to the house, which they entered, taking their several gifts back, and last of all cutting the flaps ornamented with beads away from the wife's jacket.

When the strangers were gone she said as before, "Kasiagsak has indeed been telling a lie again."

His last invention was this: he one day found a small bit of whale-skin floating on the top of the water, and bringing it home he said, "I have found the carcass of a whale; follow me and I will show it," and the boat was got out, and they started.

After a good while they asked him, "Where is it?" but he merely answered them, "Away yonder," and then a little bit further, "we shall soon get at it." But when they had gone a long way from home without seeing anything like a floating whale, they got tired of Kasiagsak, and put a stop to all his fibs by killing him then and there.

Source: Adapted from "Kasiagsak, the Great Liar," *Tales and Traditions of the Eskimo,* Henry Rink (London: William Blackwood and Sons, 1875), 291–297.

The Bad Wife

The Blackfoot shared the lifestyle of the other nomadic Plains cultures who depended on the buffalo for subsistence. Marriage among the Blackfoot was governed by strict rules of behavior, and women were expected to maintain a high degree of purity and integrity. Wives who were suspected of being unfaithful were in peril of harsh physical punishment. Therefore, to the Blackfoot the bad wife of this narrative exemplifies the moral opposite of appropriate female behavior. She is guilty of adultery, treason, cruelty, and, in her claims to supernatural powers, sacrilege. Her crimes are particularly heinous when contrasted to the old Snake (Shoshone) woman.

There was once a man who had but one wife. He was not a chief, but a very brave warrior. He was rich, too, so he could have had plenty of wives if he wished; but he loved his wife very much, and did not want any more. He was very good to this woman. She always wore the best clothes that could be found. If any other woman had a fine buckskin dress, or something very pretty, the man would buy it for her.

It was summer. The berries were ripe, and the woman kept saying to her husband, "Let us go and pick some berries for winter."

"No," replied the man. "It is dangerous now. The enemy is traveling all around." But still the woman kept teasing him to go.

So one day he told her to get ready. Some other women went, too. They all went on horseback, for the berries were a long way from camp. When they got to the place, the man told the women to keep near their horses all the time. He would go up on a butte near by and watch. "Be careful," he said. "Keep by your horses, and if you see me signal, throw away your berries, get on your horses and ride toward camp as fast as you can."

They had not picked many berries before the man saw a war party coming. He signaled the women, and got on his horse and rode toward them. It happened that this man and his wife both had good horses, but the others, all old women, rode slow old travois horses [horses used to carry burdens], and the enemy soon overtook and killed them.

Many kept on after the two on good horses, and after a while the woman's horse began to get tired; so she asked her husband to let her ride on his horse with him. The woman got up behind him, and they went on again. The horse was a very powerful one, and for a while went very fast; but two persons make a heavy load, and soon the enemy began to gain on them. The man was now in a bad plight; the enemy were overtaking him, and the woman holding him bound his arms so that he could not use his bow.

"Get off," he said to her. "The enemy will not kill you. You are too young and pretty. Some one of them will take you, and I will get a big party of our people and rescue you."

"No, no," cried the woman; "let us die here together."

"Why die?" cried the man. "We are yet young, and may live a long time together. If you don't get off, they will soon catch us and kill me, and then they will take you anyhow. Get off, and in only a short time I will get you back."

"No, no," again cried the woman; "I will die here with you."

"Crazy person!" cried the man, and with a quick jerk he threw the woman off.

As he said, the enemy did not kill her. The first one who came up counted coup and took her. The man, now that his horse was lightened, easily ran away from the war party, and got safe to camp.

Then there was great mourning. The relatives of the old women who had been killed, cut their hair and cried. The man, too, cut off his hair and mourned. He knew that his wife was not killed, but he felt very badly because he was separated from her. He painted himself black, and walked all through the camp, crying. His wife had many relations, and some of them went to the man and said: "We pity you very much. We mourn, too, for our sister. But come. Take courage. We will go with you, and try to get her back."

"It is good," replied the man. "I feel as if I should die, stopping uselessly here. Let us start soon."

That evening they got ready, and at daylight started out on foot. There were seven of them in all. The husband, five middle-aged men, the woman's relations, and a young man, her own young brother. He was a very pretty boy. His hair was longer than any other person's in camp.

They soon found the trail of the war party, and followed it for some days. At last they came to the Big River, and there, on the other side, they saw many lodges. They crept down a gully into the valley, and hid in a small stand of timber just opposite the camp. Toward evening the man said: "Kyi, my brothers. Tonight I will swim across and look all through the camp for my wife. If I do not find her, I will hide and look again tomorrow evening. But if I do not return before daylight of the second night, then you will know I am killed. Then you will do as you think best. Maybe you will want to take revenge. Maybe you will go right back home. That will be as your hearts feel."

As soon as it was dark, he swam across the river and went all about through the camp, peeping in through the doorways of the lodges, but he did not see his wife. Still, he knew she must be there. He had followed the trail of the party to this place. They had not killed her on the way. He kept looking in at the lodges until it was late, and the people let the fires go out and went to bed. Then the man went down to where the women got their water from the river. Everywhere along the stream was a cut bank, but in one place a path of steps had been made down to the water's edge. Near this path, he dug a hole in the bank and crawled into it, closing up the entrance, except one small hole, through which he could look, and watch the people who came to the river.

As soon as it was daylight, the women began to come for water. Tum, tum, tum, tum, he could hear their footsteps as they came down the path, and he looked eagerly at every one. All day long the people came and went—the young and old; and the children played about near him. He saw many strange people that day. It was now almost sunset, and he began to think that he would not see his wife there. Tum, tum, tum, tum, another woman came down the steps, and stopped at the water's edge. Her dress was strange, but he thought he knew the form. She turned her head and looked down the river, and he saw her face. It was his wife. He pushed away the dirt, crawled out, went to her and kissed her. "Kyi," he said, "hurry, and let us swim across the river. Five of your relations and your own young brother are waiting for us in that piece of timber."

"Wait," replied his wife. "These people have given me a great many pretty things. Let me go back. When it is night I will gather them up, steal a horse, and cross over to you."

"No, no," cried the man. "Let the pretty things go; come, let us cross at once."

"Pity me," said the woman. "Let me go and get my things. I will surely come tonight. I speak the truth."

"How do you speak the truth? On what do you pledge?" asked her husband.

"That my relations there across the river may be safe and live long, I speak the truth."

"Go then," said the man, "and get your things. I will cross the river now." He went up on the bank and walked down the river, keeping his face hidden. No one noticed him, or if they did, they thought he belonged to the camp. As soon as he had passed the first bend, he swam across the river, and soon joined his relations.

"I have seen my wife," he said to them. "She will come over as soon as it is dark. I let her go back to get some things that were given her."

"You are crazy," said one of the men, "very crazy. She already loves this new man she has, or she would not have wanted to go back."

"Stop that," said the husband; "do not talk bad of her. She will surely come."

The woman went back to her lodge with the water, and, sitting down near the fireplace, she began to act very strangely. She took up pieces of charred wood, dirt, and ashes in her hands and ate them, and made queer noises.

"What is it?" asked the man who had taken her for a wife. "What is the matter with you?" He spoke in signs.

The woman also spoke in signs. She answered him: "The Sun told me that there are seven persons across the river in that piece of timber. Five of them are middle-aged, another is a young boy with very long hair, another is a man who mourns. His hair is cut short."

The Snake [Blackfoot term for Shoshone] did not know what to do, so he called in some chiefs and old men to advise with him. They thought that the woman might be very strong medicine. At all events, it would be a good thing to go and look. So the news was shouted out, and in a short time all the warriors had mounted their best horses, and started across the river. It was then almost dark, so they surrounded the piece of timber, and waited for morning to begin the search.

"Kyi," said one of the woman's relations to her husband. "Did I not speak the truth? You see now what that woman has done for us."

At daylight the poor husband strung his bow, took a handful of arrows from his quiver, and said: "This is my fault. I have brought you to this. It is right that I should die first," and he started to go out of the timber.

"Wait," said the eldest relative. "It shall not be so. I am the first to go. I cannot stay back to see my brother die. You shall go out last." So he jumped out of the brush, and began shooting his arrows, but was soon killed.

"My brother is too far on the road alone," cried another relation, and he jumped out and fought, too. What use, one against so many? The Snakes soon had his scalp.

So they went out, one after another, and at last the husband was alone. He rushed out very brave, and shot his arrows as fast as he could.

"Hold!" cried the Snake man to his people. "Do not kill him; catch him. This is the one my wife said to bring back alive. See! His hair is cut short." So, when the man had shot away all his arrows, they seized and tied him, and, taking the scalps of the others, returned to camp.

They took the prisoner into the lodge where his wife was. His hands were tied behind his back, and they tied his feet, too. He could not move.

As soon as the man saw his wife, he cried. He was not afraid. He did not care now how soon he died. He cried because he was thinking of all the trouble and death this woman had caused. "What have I done to you," he asked his wife, "that you should treat me this way? Did I not always use you well? I never struck you. I never made you work hard."

"What does he say?" asked the Snake man.

"He says," replied the woman, "that when you are done smoking, you must knock the ashes and fire out of your pipe on his breast."

The Snake was not a bad-hearted man, but he thought now that this woman had strong medicine, that she had Sun power; so he thought that everything must be done as she said. When the man had finished smoking, he emptied the pipe on the Blackfoot's breast, and the fire burned him badly.

Then the poor man cried again, not from the pain, but to think what a bad heart this woman had. Again he spoke to her. "You cannot be a person," he said. "I think you are some fearful animal, changed to look like a woman."

"What is he saying now?" asked the Snake.

"He wants some boiling water poured on his head," replied the woman.

"It shall be as he says," said the Snake; and he had his women heat some water. When it was ready, one of them poured a little of it here and there on the captive's head and shoulders. Wherever the hot water touched, the hair came out and the skin peeled off. The pain was so bad that the Blackfoot nearly fainted.

When he revived, he said to his wife: "Pity me. I have suffered enough. Let them kill me now. Let me hurry to join those who have gone ahead to death."

The woman turned to the Snake chief, and said, "The man says that he wants you to give him to the Sun."

"It is good," said the Snake. "Tomorrow we move camp. Before we leave here, we will give him to the Sun."

There was an old woman in this camp who lived all alone, in a little lodge of her own. She had some friends and relations, but she said she liked to live by herself. She had heard that a Blackfoot had been captured, and went to the lodge where he was. When she saw them pour the boiling water on him, she cried and felt badly. This old woman had a very good heart. She went home and lay down by her dog, and kept crying, she felt so sorry for this poor man. Pretty soon she heard people shouting out the orders of the chief.

They said: "Listen! Listen! Tomorrow we move camp. Get ready now and pack up everything. Before we go, the Blackfoot man will be given to the Sun."

Then the old woman knew what to do. She tied a piece of buckskin around her dog's mouth, so he could not bark, and then she took him way out in the timber and tied him where he could not be seen. She also filled a small sack with pemmican, dried meat, and berries, and put it near the dog.

In the morning the people rose early. They smoothed a cotton wood tree, by taking off the bark, and painted it black. Then they stood the Blackfoot up against it, and fastened him there with a great many ropes. When they had tied him so he could not move, they painted his face black, and the chief Snake made a prayer, and gave him to the Sun.

Every one was now busy getting ready to move camp. This old woman had lost her dog, and kept calling out for him and looking all around. "Tsis'-i!" she cried. "Tsis'-i! Come here. Knock the dog on the head! Wait till I find him, and I'll break his neck."

The people were now all packed up, and some had already started on the trail. "Don't wait for me," the old woman said. "Go on, I'll look again for my dog, and catch up with you."

When all were gone, the old woman went and untied her dog, and then, going up to where the Blackfoot was tied, she cut the ropes, and he was free. But already the man was very weak, and he fell down on the ground.

She rubbed his limbs, and pretty soon he felt better. The old woman was so sorry for him that she cried again, and kissed him. Then the man cried, too. He was so glad that someone pitied him. By and by he ate some of the food the old woman had given him, and felt strong again.

He said to her in signs, "I am not done. I shall go back home now, but I will come again. I will bring all the men in my band with me, and we will have revenge."

"You say well," signed the old woman.

"Help me again," said the man. "If, on the road you are traveling, this camp should separate, mark the trail my wife takes with a stick. You, too, follow the party she goes with, and always put your lodge at the far end of the village. When I return with my people, I will enter your lodge, and tell you what to do."

"I take your speech," replied the old woman. "As you say, so it shall be." Then she kissed him again, and started on after her people. The man went to the river, swam across, and started for the North.

Why are the people crying? Why is all this mourning? Ah! The poor man has returned home, and told how those who went with him were killed. He has told them the whole story. They are getting ready for war. Everyone able to fight is going with this man back to the Snakes. Only a few will be left to guard the camp. The mother of that bad woman is going, too. She has sharpened her axe, and told what she will do when she sees her daughter. All are ready. The best horses have been caught up and saddled, and the war party has started—hundreds and hundreds of warriors. They are strung out over the prairie as far as you can see.

When they got to the Missouri River, the poor man showed them where the lodge in which they had tortured him had stood. He took them to see the tree, where he had been bound. The black paint was still on it.

From here, they went slowly. Some young men were sent far ahead to scout. The second day, they came back to the main body, and said they had found a camping place just deserted, and that there the trail forked. The poor man then went ahead, and at the forks he found a willow twig stuck in the ground, pointing to the left hand trail. When the others came up, he said to them: "Take care of my horse now, and travel slowly. I will go ahead on foot and find the camp. It must be close. I will go and see that old woman, and find out how things are."

Some men did not want him to do this; they said that the old woman might tell about him, and then they could not surprise the camp.

"No," replied the man. "It will not be so. That old woman is almost the same as my mother. I know she will help us."

He went ahead carefully, and near sunset saw the camp. When it was dark, he crept near it and entered the old woman's lodge. She had placed it behind, and a little way off from, the others. When he went in the old woman was asleep, but the fire was still burning a little. He touched her, and she jumped up and started to scream; but he put his hand on her mouth, and when she saw who it was she laughed and kissed him. "We have come," he told her. "We are going to have revenge on this camp tonight. Is my wife here?"

"Still here," replied the old woman. "She is chief now. They think her medicine very strong."

"Tell your friends and relations," said the Blackfoot, "that you have had a dream, and that they must move into the brush yonder. Have them stay there with you, and they will not be hurt. I am going now to get my people."

It was very late in the night. Most of the Snakes were in bed and asleep. All at once the camp was surrounded with warriors, shouting the war cry and shooting, stabbing, and knocking people on the head as fast as they came out of the lodges.

That Blackfoot woman, the bad wife, cried out: "Don't hurt me. I am a Blackfoot. Are any of my people here?"

"Many of your relations are here," someone said. "They will protect you."

Some young men seized and tied her, as her husband had said to do. They had hard work to keep her mother from killing her.

"Hai yah!" the old woman cried. "There is my Snake woman daughter. Let me split her head open."

The fight was soon over. The Blackfoot warriors killed the people almost as fast as they came out of their lodges. Some few escaped in the darkness. When the fight was over, the young warriors gathered up a great pile of lodge poles and brush, and set fire to it. Then the poor man tore the dress off his bad wife, tied the scalp of her dead Snake man around her neck, and told her to dance the scalp dance in the fire. She cried and hung back, calling out for pity. The people only laughed and pushed her into the fire. She would run through it, and then those on the other side would push her back. So they kept her running through the fire, until she fell down and died.

The old Snake woman had come out of the brush with her relations. Because she had been so good, the Blackfoot warriors gave her, and those with her, one-half of all the horses and valuable things they had taken.

"Kyi!" said the Blackfoot chief. "That is all for you, because you helped this poor man. Tomorrow morning we start back north. If your heart is that way, go too and live with us." So these Snakes joined the Blackfoot and lived with them until they died, and their children married with the Blackfoot, and at last they were no longer Snake people.

Source: Adapted from "The Bad Wife," *Blackfoot Lodge Tales: The Story of a Prairie People,* George Bird Grinnell (New York: Charles Scribner's Sons, 1892), pp. 39–49.

The Youth Who Joined the Deer

The term "manitou" designates a spiritual (or animating) essence that permeates humans and other living things and even some inorganic phenomena. In this case, the deer-hunter's Manitou shares similarities with the guardian spirit as used elsewhere in this collection. Among the Nlaka'pamux (or, as they are designated in the collection from which this tale was adapted, the Thompson River Indians), as is the case with many of the hunter-gatherer groups of Native America, there exists the belief that animals allow themselves to be captured or killed because of pity for humans. The generous act of the animal must be reciprocated by observing ceremonies that allow it to go to an afterlife or return to the living. The religious system described in the following tale unites humanity with those elements of the environment that allow the human community to flourish.

There was a man who was a great deer-hunter. He was constantly hunting and was very successful. He thought continually of the deer and dreamed of them. They were as friends to him. Probably they were his *manitou*. He had two wives, one of whom had borne him no children, while the other one had borne a male child.

One day while hunting, he came on the fresh tracks of a doe and fawn, which he followed. They led to a knoll on which he saw a young woman and child sitting. The tracks led directly to them. He was surprised, and asked the woman if she had seen any deer pass.

She answered, "No." He walked on, but could not find the tracks.

On his return, he said to the woman, "You must have seen the deer; the tracks seem to disappear where you are, and they are very fresh."

The woman laughed, and said, "You need not trouble yourself about the tracks. For a long time I have loved you and longed for you. Now you shall go with me to my house." They walked on together; and the hunter could not resist the attraction of the woman, nor help following her.

As he went along, he thought, "It is not well that I am acting thus. My wives and my child are at home awaiting me."

The woman knew his thoughts at once, and said, "You must not worry or think that you are doing wrong. You shall be my husband, and you will never regret it."

After the two had traveled a long way, they reached a hilly country. Then the man saw an entrance which seemed to lead underground. When they had gone some distance underground, they found themselves in a large house full of people who were just like Indians. They were of both sexes and all ages. They were well dressed in clothes of dressed skin, and wore deer-skin robes. They seemed to be very amiable and happy. As the travelers entered, some of the people said, "Our daughter has brought her husband."

That night the woman said to the hunter, "You are my husband and will sleep with me. You may embrace me, but you must not try anything else with me. You must not do so before the rutting-season. Our season comes but once a year, and lasts about a month." The hunter slept with his new wife.

On the following day the people said, "Let our son-in-law hunt. He is a great hunter. Let him get meat for us. We have no more meat." The hunter took his bow and arrows and went hunting. Two young deer, his brothers-in-law, ran ahead and stood on a knoll. Presently the hunter saw them, and killed both of them. He cut them up and carried them home leaving nothing. The chief had told him in the morning to be careful and not to throw away any part of the game.

Now the people ate and were glad. They saved all the bones and put them away in one place. They said to the hunter, "We always save every bone." When the deer were eaten, the bones were wrapped in bundles, and the chief sent a man to throw them into the water. He carried the bones of the two deer that the hunter had killed, and of another one that the people were eating when the hunter first arrived. The hunter had missed his two brothers-in-law, and thought they were away hunting. When the man who had carried the bones away returned, the two brothers-in-law and another man were with him. They had all come to life when their bones were thrown into the water.

Thus these Deer people lived by hunting and killing each other and then reviving. The hunter lived with his wife and her people and hunted whenever meat was required. He never failed to kill deer, for some of the young deer were always anxious to be killed for the benefit of the people.

At last the rutting-season came on, and the chief put the body of a large old buck on the hunter, and so transformed him into a buck. He went out with his wife and felt happy. Some other younger bucks came and fought with him and took his wife. He did not like others to have his wife; therefore he went home and felt downcast.

That night the people said, "What is the matter with our son-in-law, that he does not speak?"

Some one said, "He is downcast because a young man took his wife."

The chief said, "Do not feel sad. We shall give you medicine to wear on your body tomorrow which will make you strong, and then nobody can take your wife away from you." On the following morning he put large antlers on him, and gave him the body of a buck in its prime. That day the hunter fought off all the rival bucks and kept his wife and also all her sisters and cousins for himself. He hurt many of his brothers-in-law in fighting. The Deer people had shamans who healed the wounds of those hurt in battle, and they were busy throughout the rutting-season.

In this way they acted until the end of the rut, and the hunter was the champion during the whole season. In due time his wife gave birth to a son. When the latter was growing up, she said, "It is not fair to your people that you live entirely with my people. We should live with them for a while." She reduced a large quantity of deer-fat to the size of a handful. She did the same with a large quantity of dried venison, deerskins, and dressed buckskins.

Now she started with her child and her husband, who hunted on the way, and killed one of his brothers-in-law whenever they required food. He put the bones into the water, and they revived. They traveled along as people do; but the woman thought this too slow; therefore, they transformed themselves into deer. Now they went fast, and soon reached the country where her husband's people lived.

She said to her husband, "Do not approach the people at once, or you will die. For eight days you must prepare yourself by washing in decoctions of herbs."

Presently, they saw a young woman some distance away from the lodges. The hunter recognized her as his sister, showed himself, and called, "O sister! I have come back, but no one must come near me for eight days. After that I shall visit you; but you must clean your houses, so that there may be in them nothing old and no bad smell." The people thought him dead, and his childless wife had married again.

After the hunter had become like other people, he entered his lodge with his new wife and his son. His wife pulled out the deer-fat from under her arm, and threw it down on long feast-mats that had been spread out by the people. It assumed its proper dimensions and covered all the mats. She did the same with the dried meat and the deerskins, which almost filled a lodge. Now the people had a feast, and felt happy and pleased. The hunter stayed with his people for a considerable time. Whenever they wanted fresh meat, he gave his bow and arrows to his son and told him to hunt. The youth always took with him his half-brother, the son of his father by his Indian wife. They killed deer, for the deer were the boy's relatives and were willing to be killed. They threw the bones into the water, and the deer came back to life. The Deer-Boy taught his half-brother how to hunt and shoot deer, how to hold his bow and arrows so that he would not miss, how to cut up and preserve the meat, and he admonished him always to throw the bones into the water, so that the deer might revive.

Finally the Deer-Woman said to her husband, "We have been here now for a long time. Let us return to my people." She invited the people to accompany them, but they said they had not a sufficient number of moccasins to undertake the long journey. The woman then pulled out a parcel of dressed skins, threw it on the ground, and it became a heap of fine skins for shoes. All the women worked night and day making moccasins, and soon they were ready to start.

The first day of the journey the hunter said to his wife, "Let us send our son out, and I will shoot him." He hunted, and brought home a young deer, which the people ate. They missed the Deer-Boy, and wondered where he had gone. At night the hunter threw the bones into the water, and the boy came to life.

On the next day the hunter's wife went out, and he killed her and fed the people. They missed her, and wondered where she had gone. At night he threw the bones into the water, and she came to life. She told her husband it would be better not to continue to do this, because the people were becoming suspicious and would soon discover what they were doing. She said, "After this kill your brothers-in-law." The people traveled slowly, for there were many, and the hunter killed deer for them every day.

After many days they reached the Deer people's house. They were well received. After a time they made up their minds to return; and the Deer-Boy said he would return with his half-brother's people, and hunt for them on the way, so that they might not starve. He accompanied them to their country, and never returned.

He became an Indian and a great hunter. From him the people learned how to treat deer. He said to them, "When you kill deer, always see to it that the bones are not lost. Throw them into the water. Then the deer will come to life. A hunter who does this pleases the deer. They have affection for him, are not afraid of him, and do not keep out of his way, for they know that they will return to life whenever they give themselves into his power. The deer will always remain plentiful, because they are not really killed. If it is impossible to throw the bones into water, then burn them. Then the deer will really die, but they will not find fault with you. If a man throws deer-bones about, and takes no care of them, if he lets the dogs eat them, and people step on them, then the deer will be offended and will help him no more. They will withhold themselves, and the hunter will have no luck in hunting. He will become poor and starve."

The hunter never returned to the people. He became a deer.

Source: Adapted from "The Youth Who Joined the Deer," Stith Thompson, *Tales of the North American Indians,* (Bloomington, IN: Indiana University Press, 1929), 169–173.

The First War in the World

The following legend of the Tlingit who reside on the northwest coast of North America details the nature of their traditional warfare. Historically, warfare was conducted by large raiding parties in seagoing dugout canoes usually to capture slaves and economically valuable commodities and occasionally for revenge. Both motives are seen in this narrative. The power of shamans was utilized both offensively and to protect or warn against aggression. Villages were fortified and placed to take advantage of the natural defenses provided by the local terrain. This tale provides a particularly good example of the ways in which legends refer to well-known local landmarks to establish credibility for the events they describe.

A man named Hair-of-the-Grizzly was very fond of hunting and hunted almost every day with his brother-in-law, bringing home seal and all sorts of game that he had speared.

It was winter. One morning when he went out he speared a porpoise near the place where a devil-fish [giant octopus] lived, and began to skin it there, letting its blood spread out over the water. He told his steersman to keep a sharp lookout for the devilfish.

While they were moving along slowly skinning it, they saw the color of the devilfish coming toward them from under the water. It had its arms extended upward ready for action.

Hair-of-the-Grizzly had a big spear ready by his side, while his brother-in-law began to sharpen his knife and thought to do great things with it. When the devilfish came up out of the water he jumped into the midst of its arms along with his knife and was swallowed so quickly that he was able to do nothing; so Hair-of-the-Grizzly had to fight by himself. After he had fought with it for a long time he killed it, and the canoe began to sink with him. The canoe stood up on one end before it went under, and he climbed up on the thwarts as high as he could go. At last the devilfish went right under with them, and finally floated up again at a place called Narrow point.

Someone must have witnessed this fight, for they cut the devilfish open to see if the hunter were there, and found him stowed away snugly inside of it.

That was the man that people often talk about in these days as Hair-of-the-Grizzly. He it was who killed the devilfish.

Afterward his spirit came to one of his friends. People now try to get strength from him because he killed this devilfish. In olden times, when one killed a great creature, his strength always came to another person. Then his strength came to a certain person, impelling him to go to war.

They used to put a light, thin-skinned coat on this person's back to try his strength by endeavoring to pull it off, but they were not able to do so. They would pull this coat as far back as his shoulders, but, try as hard as they might, they could not get it farther. Then [the spirit in this shaman] told his name. He said, "I am Hair-of-the-Grizzly. I have been fought and killed a devilfish, and I come to you as a spirit." Many people came to see the shaman when he was possessed and to try him with the coat, which no one could pull off.

After his people had tested all of his spirits, they started south to war. They were always warring with the southern people. They and the southern people hated each other. When they went down with this shaman they always enslaved many women and sometimes destroyed a whole town, all on account of his strength.

There was a brave man among the southern people, who liked to kill people from up this way. One time a little boy they had captured from our people in the north escaped from the fort where this brave man was. He had a bow and arrows with him. The brave man discovered where he was, went after him, and pulled him out from under the log where he was hiding. But meanwhile the spirits in the canoes of the northern people had seen. Then the southern man took the little boy down on the beach and said to him, "Shoot me in the eye." The boy put an arrow in his bow and took such good aim that the arrow passed straight through the man's eye. The point of this arrow was made of the large mussel shell. The brave man fell just like a piece of wood thrown down. The little boy had killed him. Then all ran to the little boy and took off his head. The chiefs passed his dried scalp from one to another and wondered at what he had done. They named him ever after Little-head, and the man he killed was called One-Little-head-killed. Even now they relate how Little-head killed the brave man. Then the northern people came around the fort and destroyed everybody there, some of those in the canoes being also killed.

After that the southern people started north to war. They had a shaman among them. On the way, they came to a man named Murrelet [a small sea bird related to the auk]. When this man was young, he had been trained to run up steep cliffs by having a mountain-sheep's hoof tied to his leg or neck to give him power, and being held up to the walls of the house and made to go through the motions of climbing. They said, "Is this the man they talk about so much who can run up any mountain?" This is what they said when they were chasing him. Then they caught him and took him into one of their canoes.

Now the war chief said to his friends, "Let us take him ashore to that cliff." So they took him to a place called Bell Point, where part of the town of Huna is, to try him there. They said to him, "Murrelet, go up this cliff." When he attempted it, however, he fell back into the canoe. All the people in the canoes laughed at him. They said, "Oh! You little thing. Why is it that they say you are the best runner up this way?" After he had fallen back the third time, he said, "This is not the way I am dressed when I go up a cliff. I always carry a stone ax, a staff, and a flint, and I always carry along a seal's stomach full of grease." They prepared these things for him and gave them to him. Then he started up, wearing his claw snowshoes, which must have been shod with points as strong as the iron ones people have now. He stepped up a little distance, shook himself, and looked down. Then he called like the murrelet and went up flying.

The warriors were surprised and said, "Now give him some more things to put on his feet." They talked about him in the canoes. They said, "Look! He is up on the very top of the mountain peeping at us." Then he lit fires all along on top of the mountain. All the war canoes went along to another place where was a sandy beach.

Then they tied all the canoe ropes to the body of Murrelet's steersman, intending to use him as an anchor. Murrelet heard him crying and ran down the mountain toward him. He used his power to bring sound sleep upon his foes. As he came he made a noise like the murrelet. When he got near he told the man to cry very loudly. Probably this man was his brother. It is rather hard to say. Then he said, "I am going to cut the ropes now. Cry harder." So he cut all of the ropes, and they ran off, while the war canoes floated away. Afterward, however, the warriors found where they had drifted to and recovered them.

Then they started for the fort toward which they had originally set out and captured it. One high-caste woman, they saved and carried south. They took good care of her on account of her birth. At the time when she was captured she was pregnant, and her child was born among the southern people. They also took good care of him; and while he was growing up his mother would take some of his blood and put it upon his nose to make him brave.

For a long time he was ignorant that they were slaves, until one day a young fellow kicked his mother in the nose so that it bled. Then they told him that they were only slaves, but he said, "You people know that she is my mother. Why don't you take good care of her even if she is a slave?" After that a spirit possessed him. It was sorrow that made him have this spirit. Then he ordered them to make a paddle for him, and they made him a big one. His spirit was so very powerful that he obtained enough blankets for his services as a shaman to purchase his mother's freedom. Afterward, he got ready to come north with his stepfather and mother and they helped him to load his canoe. Before he started, his stepfather's people asked him not to bring war down upon them. No one else went with them because his spirit was going to guide them.

When they were about to start they put matting over his mother, and, whenever they were going to encamp, they never went right ashore but always dropped anchor outside. During that journey the shaman never ate.

When they came to the beach his friends did not know at first who he was, but his mother related all that had happened. Then his friends came in and began to help him show his spirits. He was getting other spirits from the country of the people he was going to war against. From his wrist up to his elbow he made as many black spots as there were towns he intended to conquer, and, while all were helping him with his spirits, the spots one after another began to smoke. His stepfather told him to remember the place where he had stayed and not destroy it. So, when the spots burned, the burning stopped at the one at his elbow, which he simply cleaned away with his hand. This meant that he would extinguish the fire at that point and not fight there.

Then all of his friends prepared themselves and set out to war. They came straight up to a certain fort without attempting to hide, and the fort people shouted, "Come on, you people." They had no iron in those days, but were armed with mussel-shell knives and spears, and wore round wooden fighting hats. They destroyed all the men at this fort and enslaved the women and children. They felt very happy over the number of people they had killed and over the number of slaves they had captured. There were no white people here then, not even Russians. It was very close to the time when Raven made us.

After that, all the southern people started north to make war, coming by the outside passage. The first place they reached while rounding this island was Murrelet Point fort. One canoe started off to spy upon them and was chased ashore but was carried across a narrow strip of land and so got back. Then they came right up to the fort, destroyed it, and captured the women. There must have been a hundred canoes coming to war. In those days, they always used bows and arrows.

A certain woman captured here said, "There is another town up the inlet from us." So they started up about evening and, when the tide was pretty well up, passed through a place where there is a small tide rip. They caught sight of the town far back inside of this and exclaimed, "There's the town." Then they landed just below it and started up into the forest in order to surround it. When it became very dark they began to make noises like birds up in the woods. In the morning they descended to fight, and the women and children began crying. They captured all. Meanwhile the tidal rapids began to roar as the tide fell.

One woman among the captives was very old. They asked her what time of tide to run the rapids, and she said to herself, "It is of no use for me to live, for all of my friends and brothers are gone. It is just as well to die as to be enslaved." So she said to them, "At half tide."

Then two canoes started down ahead in order to reach some forts said to lie in another direction. They rushed straight under when the rapids rose and were seen no more. The old woman was drowned with them. So they made a mark with their blood at the place where these two canoe loads had been drowned to tell what had happened. It may be seen today and looks like yellowish paint.

Next day the remaining canoes started out when the tide was high and came to another fort next morning. While they were around behind this a woman came out. Then they seized her and ran a spear into her body many times until she dropped dead without speaking. Then the people fought with clubs and bows and arrows until all in the fort were destroyed and started on to another. When they made an attack in those days, they never approached in the daytime but toward dawn when everybody was sleeping soundly. Both sides used wooden helmets and spears.

At this fort, the women were always digging a big variety of clam, storing these clams in the fort for food. The fort was filled with them. So, when the assailants started up the cliff, one of the men inside struck him with a clam shell just under the war hat so that he bled profusely. He could not see on account of the blood. Then the man in the fort took an Indian ax and beat out his brains. Afterward all in the fort seized clam shells and struck their foes in the face with them so that they could not come up. They threw so fast that the canoes were all kept away; so, that place is now called Where-clams-kept-out-the-foes. For the same reason this was the only fort where any people were saved, and on the other hand, many of the enemy were destroyed by the fort people.

Now they left this fort and came to another, landing on a beach near by, and between them and the fort was what they supposed to be a fresh water pond. Then one of them called Little-Bear-Man, because he had on a bear-skin coat, began to shoot at the fort with arrows. But the people in the fort shouted to him, "Do not be in such great haste. The tide runs out from the place where you are."

Then the bear man said, "The people here say that the tide runs out from this place, but [I know] that it is a freshwater pond." Presently the tide began to run out from it as they had told him, so he chopped some wood, made a fire and lay by it to wait. After the tide had ebbed, they began to fight, destroyed everybody there, and burned the fort down. Close by the site of this fort is a place called Porpoise-belly.

The warriors thought they were getting much the best of the people up this way, but really only a few were left to look after the forts, most being collected elsewhere.

After they had destroyed all the people in four forts they landed on a long sandy beach to cut off the scalps. When there was no time to scalp, the heads were carried away until there should be more leisure. Scalps and slaves were what people fought for, and they dried the scalps by rubbing them on hot stones or holding them near the fire. Then they again started north. This raid consumed the whole summer.

Southward was a fort on a high cliff, called Jealous-man fort. It was named this because the man who encamped there was so jealous of his wife that he would let no one else live near him. When the foes all stopped in front of him, and he could hear them talking, he began to quarrel with them, saying, "You big round heads, you want to destroy all of the people up this way." While they were talking back at him one of their canoes struck a rock and split in two, and, after they had rescued the people in it, they began talking about this circumstance, saying, "If we wait any longer he will quarrel us over as well." So they left him and went on north.

The next fort they attacked was called Huna-people's fort, and it stood just where they were going to turn south again. Here they had the greatest fight of all, and the fort people killed many of them. Finally, they broke up all the canoes of these people and started south. At this time, they were overloaded with the slaves they had taken, but they went in to every fort they passed near and broke up the canoes belonging to it. The last of these forts was called Fort-that-rapids-run-around. When they had destroyed all of the canoes there, they said, "Will you people bring any more wars upon us? You will not dare to fight us again." They felt very happy, for they thought that they had destroyed all of the northern people, and that no more raids would be made upon them.

Most of the northern people, however, were encamped along the coast to the westward, and, when they heard what had happened, they came from all over. They talked together for a long time and finally decided upon a plan. All the men began to sharpen their stone axes, and, when that was finished, they came to a big tree they had already marked out and began to chop at it from all sides. This was the biggest tree ever known. While they worked, the women would come around it wailing and mourning for their dead friends. It took two days to chop this tree down, and, if anybody broke his stone ax, they felt very sorry for him and beat the drums as though some one were dead. Then, they cut the tree in two and took a section off along the whole length where the upper side of the canoe was to be, and the head workman directed that it be burnt out inside with fire. So all the people assembled about it to work, and as fast as it was burnt they took sticks and knocked off the burnt part so as to burn deeper and to shape it properly when it had been burned enough. This work took them all winter. During the same time they bathed in the sea and whipped one another in order to be brave in the approaching war.

Toward spring they got inside of the canoe with their stone axes and began to smooth it by cutting out the burnt part. Then they began to give names to the canoe. It was finally called Spruce-canoe. Finally they finished it by putting in seats.

Now they were only waiting for it to get warmer. In those days there were special war leaders, and in fighting they wore helmets and greaves made of common varieties of wood.

There was a shaman among these people Because they were going to war, all of his people would come about him to help him capture the souls of the enemy.

One time he said to his servant, "Go out for food, and be brave. The head spirit is going to help you." So the servant went out as directed and the spirit showed him the biggest halibut in the ocean. For the float to his line he used the largest sea-lion stomach, and, when he began to pull it up, it looked as though the whole ocean were flowing into its mouth. But the shaman told him to be courageous and hold on though the hook looked like nothing more than a small spot. It did not even move, for the strength of the spirits killed it, but it was so large that they had to tow it in below the town. Then all the people who were going to fight cut the halibut up and began to dry it. There was enough for all who were going to war and for all the women left at home. When it was dried they started to pack part away in the canoe. Then they pushed the canoe down on skids made of the bodies of two women whom they had captured from the southern people on a previous expedition and whom they now killed for the purpose. Meanwhile, the southern people thought that they had destroyed all of those at the north and were scattered everywhere in camps, not taking the trouble to make forts.

Finally, all the northern warriors got into the big canoe and they started south. It took probably ten days to get there. At the first camp they reached, they killed all who were there, except for a few women. Of one woman who was saved they asked where the other people were, and she said that they were scattered everywhere in camps which she named. After they had destroyed the second camp they enslaved more women. Then they asked the woman, "Didn't you expect any war party to come down here?"

She said, "No one expected another raid down here, so they built no forts."

The big canoe went around everywhere, killing people, destroying property, and enslaving women. The women captured at each place told them where others were to be found, and so they continued from place to place. They destroyed more of the southern people than were killed up this way. When they thought that they had killed everybody they started north.

Then they reached home, and everybody felt happy. They not only brought numbers of slaves but liberated those of their own people who had been taken south. Since that time people have been freer to camp where they please, and, although the northern and southern people fought against each other for a long time, more slaves were taken up this way, so the northern people did not esteem the southern people very highly. This is said to have been the very oldest war.

Source: Adapted from "The First War in the World," *Tlingit Myths and Texts.* John R. Swanton. Smithsonian Institution Bureau of American Ethnology Bulletin 39, (Washington, D.C.: Government Printing Office, 1909), pp. 72–79.

The Medicine Pipe

The Teton were the major division of the Dakota (Sioux) residing in the northern plains in pursuit of the buffalo herds that provided their major source of subsistence. The following narrative justifies the power of Dakota ritual and connects this ritual object to an important event in the tensions between Native Americans and the United States Army.

W hen the Indians were all living together in the east, near a great lake, they were encamped in a large circle. At that time, there was supposed to be but one language spoken; and there were chiefs for every tribe, one chief to every band.

One day two young men went out hunting in a mountainous country. At the top of a high tableland they found game.

On their way down the hill they saw a woman coming toward them. As they came near to the woman they noticed that she had something in her arms. On approaching still nearer they discovered that she was a fine-looking young woman, carrying a pipe on her left arm. Suddenly one of the young men said: "Let us approach her."

The other man, who said: "No, it is not well that you should do anything of the sort, for she is of mysterious appearance." When they came closer, both men stopped and obstructed her way.

The woman stopped and said: "I heard what you were saying." The woman said: "I do not wish to stir up any strife, since I am on a special errand from the Great Medicine." With this she stepped aside, took the pipe, which was seen to be filled, from her left arm and laid it down upon a buffalo chip, with the stem directly toward the east. Then she laughed and sat down.

The tempter approached her abruptly and threw her down. Then, there seemed to be a very great rumbling in the heavens, and there came forth from the heavens, as it were, mist which enveloped the place where they lay so that they could not be seen. There they remained for a time, and when the mist lifted there was to be seen only the skeleton of the man, but the woman came away unchanged.

The young man who had stood at one side watching was frightened and started to run away, but the woman called him back. As he looked back the woman told him to go to the camp where all the people were and say, "A sacred pipe is coming to you, which will furnish you abundance in the Spirit Land."

The young man went away as fast as he could, and when he came to the place of the chief he delivered his message. Immediately all the chiefs were gathered together, and they erected a tipi large enough to contain a great many people, and they made ready for the-coming of the woman with the pipe.

As she appeared on the hilltop on her way to the camp, the lightning flashed in every direction about her. So mysterious was her coming that even the dogs were afraid to bark. As the woman drew near, the chiefs gathered in a circle, holding in their midst a red blanket, with a white border and thus they went forth to meet her. A little distance from the camp the woman stopped, and when the priests came to her they threw down the blanket for her to stand upon. All of the chiefs took hold of the blanket and carried her to the center of the large tipi especially prepared for her coming.

The woman had with her the large pipe, and when she was set down, she spoke as follows, "This pipe is to be transmitted from generation to generation, and thus it shall be handed down to the end of time." The woman laid the pipe on a buffalo chip. Again she spoke, and said, "There shall be but one nation, and by that nation this pipe must be kept sacred; it must be used in time of war, in time of famine, in time of sickness, in time of need of any sort, as an instrument for preservation. This pipe will be your chief deity. It must be kept by the best chief of the tribe, and must be attended to once a year, by the assemblage of the most upright chiefs. Whenever they open the pipe there must be made tools expressly for handling the fire, a certain stick must be trimmed and handled by virgins or by young men of chastity, expressly for the pipe, a tamper, and a little spoon must be made to take up the fire. The pipe must have a wrapping of wool of the buffalo only. From the first enemy that shall be killed through the power of the pipe an ear shall be cut off and tied to the pipe-stem. The first scalp to be taken shall be treated in the same way. Whenever you are hungry my instructions must be followed. Ten men shall open the pipe, to plead to the Great Owner of the pipe. Should the man holding the pipe do any wrong there would be a demolition of his whole family. Through the advice of your ten best chiefs the pipe shall be kept by the very best chief of all. As long as the holder shall walk reverently and keep himself in order, the keeping of the pipe shall be hereditary."

As the woman was leaving the tipi she said that she was going to stop four times on the way to the hill, and the priests should smoke the pipe as she was leaving; that the fourth time she should stop she would transform herself. The ten chiefs lighted the pipe, and as they were smoking the woman went away, then stopped and looked back. Again she went on, and looked back. Again she stopped and looked back, and the fourth time she stopped and looked back she turned toward the hill and ran, and she transformed herself into a splendid five-year-old buffalo, then disappeared in the hills.

Now the chiefs assembled and held a council, so as to establish rules regulating the keeping of the pipe. They selected the best chief to hold the pipe. During the ceremony of the pipe he was to relate exactly the story that the woman had told when she brought the pipe to the camp, nor might he deviate from or leave out any of her words. While the chiefs were still in council they secured a wrapper for the pipe, also all the sticks that were necessary for use with the pipe, all made by maidens. The pipe was then raised high aloft in the midst of the council lodge. The pipe was cared for with great reverence.

A few days after the pipe had been brought, there was a quarrel within the camp in which two people were killed. In accordance with the woman's command, they cut the ear from one and tied it on the pipe-stem, together with the scalp, and that ear and that scalp are on the pipe to this day. The same sticks that were made by the ancient people, as also the covering of buffalo hair, are still with the ancient pipe, which is said to be nine hundred years old.

This pipe is now kept by an old Teton Sioux chief who lives at the Cheyenne Agency, South Dakota, and who is about ninety-three years old. They say that when he dies he will have been the last man to hold the pipe; that he is to go to the grave with the pipe.

There have been offerings made to this pipe by different tribes, such as bracelets, earrings, rings, arrows, brushes, stones, and various other trinkets being given to the pipe alone, all of which are kept with the pipe. They say that whenever in need or hungry, the buffalo gone, they go to work and call the ten best men in, who go and plead to the pipe, having unwrapped it, and that within from one to three days thereafter they receive all that they pray for. Since the scattering of the tribe, in times of peace the pipe is held as peacemaker, and hence is sometimes called the "pipe of peace," but the people call it the "calf pipe," for the woman who brought it transformed herself into a buffalo, and the pipe coming from her must therefore be a calf.

General Custer swore by this pipe that he was not going to fight the Indians any more. But the very next summer he met death, for he disregarded the oath he had made to the pipe. He who swears by the pipe and breaks oath, comes to destruction, and his whole family dies, or sickness comes upon them.

Source: Adapted from. "Legend of the Teton Sioux Medicine Pipe." George A. Dorsey, *Journal of American Folklore*, 19 (1906): 326–329.

Little Warrior's Counsel

With the appearance of Europeans in the Americas and the ensuing tensions between the new arrivals and Native Americans, armed conflicts were common. However, as in the following historical narrative of Little Warrior, a college-educated Pawnee, there were important exceptions to this rule, cases in which diplomacy rather than violence won the day.

Most of the Pawnee heroes are so admired because of victories, daring deeds, the coups they have counted and the horses they have stolen. The glory of Comanche Chief and of Lone Chief depends mainly on their bravery, rather than on the fact that they were peace makers. Yet, there should be room among these stories for the account of an educated Pawnee a man who by his wise counsel to a warrior of a hostile tribe saved many lives, both of Indians and of white men.

Little Warrior was educated at a Western college, but has shown his bravery on the field of battle, and has sacrificed a scalp to Ti-ra'-wa [Pawnee Supreme Being]. In the year 1879, at the time of the Ute outbreak, after Major Thornburgh's command had been annihilated, Little Warrior was employed as a scout for the US Army troops.

On the headwaters of the Arkansas River he was one day scouting in advance of the command, in company with four white soldiers and four Indian scouts. This day, the party saw far off on the prairie an Indian, who showed a white flag, and came toward them. When he had come near to them, the soldiers proposed to kill him, and report that he was a Ute, one of the Indians that they were looking for.

But Little Warrior said, " No. He has a white flag up, and it may be that he is carrying a dispatch, or, perhaps, he is a white man disguised as an Indian."

When the man had come close to them, they saw that he was dressed like a Comanche; he did not have the bristling fringe of hair over the forehead that the Utes wear, and his side locks were unbraided. Little Warrior asked him, by signs, if he were alone, to which he replied in the same sign language that he was alone. Then Little Warrior inquired who he was. The stranger made the sign for Comanche, a friendly tribe.

They took him into the camp, and after a while Little Warrior began to talk to him in Comanche. He could not understand a word of it.

Then the Pawnee said to him, "My friend, you are a Ute."

The stranger acknowledged that he was.

Then Little Warrior talked to him, and gave him much good advice. He said, "My friend, you and I have the same skin, and what I tell you now is for your good. I speak to you as a friend, and what I say to you now is so that you may save your women and your children. It is of no use for you to try to fight the white people. I have been among them, and I know how many they are. They are like the grass. Even if you were to kill a hundred it would be nothing. It would be like burning up a few handfuls of prairie grass. There would be just as many left. If you try to fight them they will hunt you like a ghost. Wherever you go they will follow after you, and you will get no rest. The soldiers will be continually on your tracks. Even if you were to go up on top of a high mountain, where there was nothing but rocks, and where no one else could come, the soldiers would follow you, and get around you, and wait, and wait, even for fifty years. They would have plenty to eat, and they could wait until after you were dead. There is one white man who is the chief of all this country, and what he says must be done. It is no use to fight him."

"Now," Little Warrior continued, "if you are wise you will go out and get all your people, and bring them in, on to the reservation, and give yourself up. It will be better for you in the end. I speak to you as a friend, because we are both the same color, and I hope that you will listen to my words."

The Ute said, " My friend, your words are good, and I thank you for the friendly advice you have given me. I will follow it and will agree to go away and bring in my people."

Little Warrior said, " How do you make a promise?"

The Ute said, " By raising the right hand to One Above."

Little Warrior said, "That is the custom also among my people."

The Ute raised his hand and made the promise.

After he had been detained two or three weeks, he was allowed to go, and about a month afterward, he brought in the band of which he was chief, and surrendered. Through his influence afterward, the whole tribe came in and gave themselves up. He was grateful to Little Warrior for what he had done for him, and told him that if he ever came back into his country he would give him many ponies.

Source: Adapted from "Little Warrior's Counsel," *Pawnee Hero Stories and Folktales.* George Bird Grinnell. (New York: Charles Scribner's Sons, 1893), pp. 79–83

The Tricky Medicine Man

In the following tale, a Navaho healer resorts to theft in order to survive. He hides his crime behind his legitimate profession of singer, so-called because the curing process, in part, requires the singing of long portions of Navaho myth over the body of the patient. The narrator excuses this crime by asserting that harsh conditions in the recent past forced even people with an honest means of making a living into occasional deviations from proper conduct.

The story that I am going to tell will probably give a brief idea of what the Navahos had faced long ago. It was mostly survival for whatever food that can sustain them through their lives, and wherever it was possible, of course they went out hunting for deer and wild turkey and other animals that were edible.

But this story is about a medicine man and his nephew. He very seldom got business. When he did get business to perform a ceremony at somebody's place, why, he generally asked for something to eat, which would be a sheep, so that he would have some meat to eat. But in this case, for a long time, for several weeks, he did not have anybody to call him to help them with the healing.

So one afternoon he decided, he said: "My nephew," he said, "that family over there, they have plenty of sheep. And I think that tonight we'd better make a raid on them somehow. So go get the horses."

So he sent his nephew out, and he brought the horses and he saddled them up, ready for the night when the sheep were all in the pen. And after about eleven o'clock, they started.

"Well," he figured, "everyone should be sleeping by now over there." They went over there. And sure enough, the sheep were all penned up.

They hid the horses further back in the woods and from there they went on foot. They walked. They walked over there, and a dog started barking at them. And then they said, "Well, we'd better lay low for a while, until that quiets down." So, after a while, the dog quieted down. Then they started off to the sheep pen again.

And one climbed over the fence. He said, "I'll try and get a big one. You stand and wait outside." So he went. Just when he was climbing over the fence, why, there was a great big sheep there. So he grabbed it, and he said, "Here now, let's hurry and get out of this place."

So they grabbed it, and each of them holding the legs, why, they started running through the woods. They came back to their horses, and they tied the sheep up, and put it in front of their saddle. And from there they took off. By the time they took off, the dog was barking. But it was too late.

Anyway they got home. They penned the sheep up for the rest of the night, and they went to sleep.

Early in the morning they got up when it was about dawn. And they said, "Well, I think we'd better butcher this right away." So they did. They butchered it, and fixed up all the intestines and other things like all of us Navahos do. We cook every bit of the insides out in the coals and eat them up. Anyway, they did not let anything go to waste. They used every bit of it.

The rest of the meat they had to cut up and dry so they set around between the trees a rope or wire and they hung up all the rest of the meat to dry.

While the meat was all drying, why, this old man went up on the hill. He was out for a walk late in the afternoon. He saw somebody. He said, "It looks like somebody is coming this way." And he saw three people coming. It was quite a long distance and he knew how long it took riding on a horse to travel that distance. So he hurried back to the hogan [dome-shaped Navajo dwelling] and he called his nephew.

And he said, "Come here. I am afraid we're being tracked, because of what we did the other night." So he said, "Well, I've got a good plan." And he said, "Now you go and you're going to be the patient. And I'm going to be the medicine man. I'll tell a story. You don't say anything, but you just lie down there on that sheepskin." And so he said, "All right, let's hurry. But first of all we've got to disguise everything. Get a sack, and get all that meat that was drying out there off the lines as fast as you can."

So they hustled around as fast as they could and got all the meat and every evidence revealing where they butchered and everything was covered up.

"Well, anyway," the uncle said, "the next thing we'd better do is to get some branches of cedar and other herbs that we'll pretend are part of a real ceremony now. And when they come and question us on anything, why, we have a good story to tell. And they will never suspect us and they'll just go on and try to hunt whoever the thief is." And so they hurried and hustled around and got everything ready.

Well, by that time he looked up again and the riders had crossed the valley and were coming up the hill a little bit. And then he said, "Well, I'm going to start singing this chant, and it'll be about four verses before they get here so it'll take quite a while. And so he started his chant and he said, "The only thing that I want you to do is to groan once in a while. Now pretend that you are hurt somewhere outside here and I'm trying to get you well. Have this band tied around your waist just as tight as you can stand it and we'll put some branches in between for your healing."

His nephew went to bed. And the uncle said, "All I want you to do is to groan every now and then. And complain of pain."

So the medicine man was singing away. He got his medicine bag outside and scattered it in front, inside the hogan. And he was singing away. Just about the time when he came to the fifth verse, why, the people came walking in. He did not pay attention to them. He just kept singing. He was so serious in what he was doing that he forgot that these people had walked in.

After he got through with the fifth verse he says, "Nobody is to walk outside. This is a very sacred ceremony we're having. I've got another whole verse to sing and nobody steps outside until I've sprinkled the corn pollen for the ceremony." So he starts singing again. By that time these riders were getting tired.

They said, "Oh, how, oh why did we have to come in? Oh, dear. How long do we have to wait? How long is he going to keep this up?" So they were getting rather impatient but the medicine man paid no attention. He just kept on singing till he finished the sixth verse.

And then he turned around. He said, "Well, I guess now we are through." And he sprinkled his medicine pollen, and he said, "Now, what did you people come for? I was wondering. I hope that you came after me to do some singing or want me to practice some of the ceremonies, but I'm busy right now, I'll have to finish the business I have now, but I'll be through in another two or three days. I'll be through," he told them.

And then the man who was the leader of the riders spoke up. He said, "No, we didn't come after you to do any singing, but we came to ask some questions. The night before last somebody stole one of our big sheep over there out of the corral. I wonder if you have seen anybody riding. We found two horse tracks and two sets of footprints by the corral. And that's the night that the dog was barking, but nobody went outside to see what was going on. And we just came to ask that question."

And the medicine man said, "I don't know. I didn't see anybody."

Then they said that "the track came this way." So that was what they were trailing.

"Well," he said, "we've been busy for almost two days now. The day before we were down there working on the fence. That's when my nephew got hurt."

By that time his nephew was just groaning with pain, and he tried to sound like he was just in terrific agony and squirming around on the sheepskin.

He said, "Ouch, it's hurting so badly!"

And he says, "See, we're busy here and he got hurt while we were trying to fix the fence. One of those logs fell on him. And I'm sorry, I can't help you, and I didn't see any of those people whoever they are. Maybe at the next camp they could tell you if they had seen anybody. But as far as we know, we don't know anything about it. If it happened at night, why, we were either asleep or getting our ceremony here, so if anybody passed by that's probably when it took place."

"Well, thank you for answering our questions. We shall go on," the visitors said. They got back on their horses and they went on again, trying to find out who stole their sheep.

Anyway, after a while the medicine man goes out. He says, "I got to get some fresh air." So he's outside up on the hill. When he knew that they were quite a ways out of sight and would not return, why, he came back to the hogan.

He says to his nephew, "You crazy thing, get up, and take all those things off, and build a fire and let's get some food cooked here!" So his nephew got up and gathered some wood. They started cooking the meat that they had stolen the night before.

This is the story of long ago when the Navahos really had a hard time, and they had to live one way or the other to survive, either to steal or to get it in a decent way. Why, medicine men were considered quite lucky because they knew how to earn their way through. But in a case like this, why, I guess he had to use both ways in order to survive.

Source: Adapted from "The Tricky Medicine Man," "Four Navaho Summer Tales: Part II," Herbert J. Landar, *Journal of American Folklore,* 72 (1959): 248–251, pp. 248–50.

THE SUPERNATURAL

How Glooskap Made a Magician of a Young Man, Who Aided Another to Win a Wife

Glooskap is an important trickster figure and culture hero among the Micmac and other Algonquian peoples of New England. Unlike many mythic characters, Glooskap was believed to maintain an ongoing interaction with human beings and occasionally to bestow his magical power on mortals, as in the following narrative.

It is well known to all Indians who still keep the true faith of the olden time that there are wondrous dwellers in the lonely woods that the Micmacs call "Mikumwess."

These can work great wonders and also sing so as to charm the wildest beasts. From them alone come the magic pipes or flutes, which sometimes pass into possession of noted sorcerers and great warriors; and when these are played upon, the woman who hears the melody is bewitched with love, and the moose and caribou follow the sound even to their death. When the Mikumwesses are pleased with a mortal they make him a magical being, even like themselves.

In old times there was an Indian village, and in it were two young men, who had heard that Glooskap, ere he left the world, would bestow on those who came to him whatever they wanted. So they went their way, an exceeding long pilgrimage, until they came to a great island, where he dwelt. And there they first met with Bear and Marten, and next with the Glooskap himself. Then they all, sitting down to supper, had placed before them only one extremely small dish, and on this there was a tiny bit of meat, and nothing more. But being a bold and jolly fellow, the first of the young Micmacs, thinking himself mocked for sport, cut off a great part of the meat, and ate it, when that which was in the dish grew in a twinkling to its former size; and so this went on all through the supper, every one eating his fill, the dish at the end being as full as ever.

Of these two, one wished to become a Mikumwess, and the other to win a very beautiful girl, the daughter of a great chief, who imposed such cruel tasks on all who came for her, that they died in attempting them.

And the first was taken by Glooskap; and after he had by a merry trick covered him with filth and put him to great shame, he took him to the river, and after washing him clean and combing his hair gave him a change of raiment and a hair string of exceeding great magic virtue, since when he had bound it on he became a Mikumwess, having all the power of the spirit-world. And also because he desired to excel in singing and music, the Master gave him a small pipe, and it was that which charmed all living beings; and then singing a song bade him join in with him. And doing this he found that he could sing, and ever after had a wondrous voice.

Now to seek the beautiful girl it was necessary to sail afar over the sea; and during this adventure the Mikumwess was charged to take care of the younger pilgrim. So he begged the Master to lend him his canoe. And Glooskap answered, "Yes, I will do this for thee, if you will honestly return it when you need it no more. Yet in very truth I did never yet lend it to mortal man but that I had to go after it myself."

Thereupon the young man promised most faithfully that he would indeed return the canoe, and with this they got them ready for the journey. But when they came to the bay there was no canoe, and they knew not what was to be done. But Glooskap pointed to a small island of granite which rose amid the waves, and it was covered with tall pine-trees. "There is my canoe!" said he; and when he had taken them unto it, it became a real canoe, with masts, and they set sail on it, rejoicing.

So they came in time to a very large island, where they drew up the canoe and hid it in the bushes. Then they went forward to seek for people, and found a village in which dwelt the chief who had the beautiful daughter, in seeking whom so many had lost their lives.

And having found him, they went into his wigwam, and were placed on the seat of honor. Now when a Micmac seeks a wife, he or his mutual friend makes no great ado about it, but utters a few words, which tell the whole story. And these are *"Sewin-coadoo-gwahloogwet"* which mean in Micmac, "I am tired of living alone." And the chief, hearing this, consented that the young man should marry her whom he sought, but on one condition, and this was that he should slay and bring to him the head of a certain horned serpent who lived a great distance away. So this was agreed upon, and the two strangers went to the wigwam, which was assigned for them.

Now in the night he that was Mikumwess arose and went alone and afar until he came to the den of the dragon, and this was a great hole in the ground. And over this he laid a mighty log, and then began the magic dance around the den. So the great serpent, hearing the call, came forth, putting out his head after the manner of snakes, waving it all about in every way and looking round him. While doing this he rested his neck upon the log, when the Indian with a blow of his hatchet severed it. Then taking the head by one of the shining yellow horns he bore it to his friend, who in the morning gave it to the chief. And the old man said to himself, "This time I fear me I shall lose my child."

Yet the young man had more to do; for the chief said, "I would desire to see my son coast down yonder hill on a hand-sled." Now this hill was an exceeding high mountain; the sides were ragged with rocks and terrible with trees and ice. Then two toboggans were brought out, one of them for the two strangers, and this he that was Mikumwess was to direct. And on the other were two powerful men, and these were both shamans who hoped to see the former soon fall out, and then to run over them. And at the word they went flying fearfully down the mountain, and yet ever faster, as if to death. And soon he that sought the girl went whirling headlong from the sled, and the two shamans gave a loud hurrah; for they did not know that this had been done with intent by the Mikumwess, that he might get them before him. So he put forth his hand, and, seizing the younger man, turned a little aside, but in an instant went on after; and soon the sled of the shamans stopped, but the other, bounding upward from a mighty wall of ice, flew far over their heads onward; nor did it stop in the valley, but, running with tremendous speed up the opposite hill and into the village, struck the side of the chief's wigwam, ripping it up from end to end before it stopped.

And the old man, seeing this, said, "This time I have lost my daughter!"

Yet the young man had more to do; for the chief said, "There is here a man who has never been beaten in running, and you must strive with him in that and overcome him, to win your wife." And the race was appointed; but before it came off he that was Mikumwess lent to his friend the magic pipe to give him power.

And when he that was the racer of the village met the young man, the youth said, "Who are you?" and he replied, "I am the Northern Lights [aurora borealis], but who are you?"

And he answered, "I am the Chain Lightning."

And they ran. In an instant they were no longer in sight; they were far away over the most distant hills. Then all sat and waited, and before it was noon he that was the Chain Lightning returned, and he was not out of breath, nor weary, and he had gone round the world. And at evening they saw the Northern Lights return, and he trembled and quivered with fatigue; yet for all that he had not been round the world, but had turned back. And the old chief, seeing him beaten, exclaimed, "This time I shall lose my child!"

And yet there was another trial of the young man before he could win her whom he wanted. For the chief had a man who no one could overcome in swimming and diving. And the young man must strive with him.

And when they met he asked the man of the village his name, and he replied, "I am Sea Duck, but who are you?"

And he answered, "I am Loon."

So they dived, and after a time Sea Duck rose again for breath, but those who waited, waited long indeed before they saw the Loon. And an hour passed, and he came not, and yet another, ere they beheld him; but when he at last rose the old chief said, "This is the end of all our weary work, for this time truly I have lost my child."

Yet it was not the end of the wonderful deeds, which were done in that village by the power of the great Glooskap. For the Mikumwess, at the great dance, which was held that evening at the wedding, astonished all who beheld him. As he danced around the circle, upon the very hard beaten floor, they saw his feet sink deeper at every step, and ever deeper as the dance went on; ploughing the ground up into high, uneven ridges, forming a trench as he went, until at length only his head was to be seen. And this ended the dancing for that night, since the ground was no longer to be danced upon by anybody except wizards and witches.

Then the young man and his wife and the Mikumwess entered their canoe and sailed homeward. And yet their trials were not over. For they had not gone far before they saw an awful storm coming to meet them; and he that had the magical spells knew that it was raised by sorcery, since these storms are the worst of all. Then, without fear, he rose, and, filling his lungs and puffing his cheeks, he blew against the tempest, wind against wind, until he blew the wind away, and the great water was as calm and smooth as before.

So they sailed on over the sunlit sea, but it was not long before the Micmac magician saw rising among the waves far before them a dark mass, which soon proved to be a tremendous beast coming to attack them. And as he drew near they saw it was the giant beaver, and his eyes were angry. But the Mikumwess, seeing this, steered straight to meet the monster, and, coming to him, said, "I am the great hunter of beavers; lo, I am their butcher; many a one has fallen by my hand." Now the Beaver had placed himself under water, with his tail out of it and rising upward, that he might sink the canoe with a single blow; for the Beaver strikes mightily in such a way. But the youth with the magic power, with one blow of his tomahawk, cut the tail from the body, and sailed onward.

Yet they had not gone far before, on rounding a point, they saw before them another animal of giant size, who likewise had his tail in the air, waiting to overcome them, and this was the giant skunk. Yet before he made his hideous attack the Mikumwess, ever on the watch, caught up his spear, and, hurling it, pierced the monster, who did but kick two or three times ere he died. And, stepping ashore, he who had slain him took a pole, a long dead pine, which lay upon the sand, and, impaling the Skunk, lifted him high in air, and, planting the tree on the ground, left him, saying scornfully, as he left, " And now show your tail there!"

So they returned safely. And Glooskap met them at the landing, and his first words were, "Well, my friends, I see that you have brought back my canoe."

And they answered, "We have, indeed."

Then he inquired, "Has all gone well with you?" And they replied that it had. Then Glooskap, laughing, let them know that in all they had experienced he had been busy, and that in all their triumphs he had had a hand. And to the Mikumwess he said, "Go now your way, you and these others, and ever lead happy lives: you amid the magical beings, they among mankind. And be sure of this, that if danger or trouble should come to you, you have but to think of me, and verily aid will come." So they rose and went to their homes.

Source: Adapted from "How Glooskap Made a Magician of a Young Man, Who Aided Another to Win a Wife and do Wonderful Deeds," *The Algonquin Legends of New England.* Charles G. Leland. (New York: Houghton, Mifflin and Company, 1884), pp. 82–92.

Tijaiha the Sorceror

In this legend of the Hurons of the northeastern woodlands, Tijaiha distorts cultural tradition to his own ends. His encounter with the horned water serpent mirrors the vision quest. The power to defeat one's enemies is a common reward, but the serpent's request for the sacrifice of a family member is abnormal. Not only does Tijaiha practice sorcery, a heinous crime to traditional Hurons, he betrays his village and his kin by allying himself with the enemy Iroquois.

When the French came (so the chief's words were rendered) the missionaries tried to prevail on the Indians to receive their religion. They asked the Indians if they knew anything about God. The Indians replied that they did; that three or four times a year they had meetings, at which the women and children were present, and then the chiefs told them what to do and warned them against evil practices. The missionaries said that this was good, but that there was a better way, which they ought to know. They ought to become Christians.

But the Indians said, "We have many friends among the creatures about us. Some of us have snake friends, some eagles, some bears, and the like. How can we desert our friends?"

The priests replied, "There is only one God."

"No," said the Indians, "there are two gods, one for the Indians and the other for the whites."

The discussion lasted three days. Finally, the priests said it was true, there were two Gods, Jesus and the Holy Ghost. One of these might be the same as the Indian God. The Indians could follow all his commands which were good, and also obey the commands of Jesus. But they would have to give up their allies among the brutes. Some of the Hurons became Christians, but others refused to accept the new religion. Among these was a noted warrior, a young man, named Tijaiha.

On one occasion he left the town with his family to hunt on the Huron River. One day, coming to a deep pool near the river, he beheld a violent commotion in the water, which was evidently made by a living creature. Of what nature it might be he did not know, though he believed it to be a great serpent, and to be possessed, like many of the wild creatures, of supernatural powers. Thereupon, after the fashion of the Indians, he fasted for ten days, eating occasionally only a few morsels to preserve life; and he prayed to the creature that some of its power might be bestowed on him. At the end of the tenth day a voice from the disturbed pool demanded what he wanted. He replied that he wanted to have such power given to him that he could vanquish and destroy all his enemies. She (the creature) replied that this power should be conferred upon him if he would grant her what she desired. He asked what this was, and was told that she would require one of his children. If he would grant this demand, he might come at night and learn from her the secret which would give him the power he sought for. He objected to this sacrifice, but offered, in place of the child, to give an old woman, his wife's mother. (Mrs. White translated this unfilial proposition with an expression of quizzical humor). The creature accepted the substitute, and the bargain was concluded.

That night Tijaiha returned to the pool, and learned what he had to do. He was to prepare a cedar arrow, with which he must shoot the creature when she should appear, at his call, above the water. From the wound he could then draw a small quantity of blood, the possession of which would render him invincible, and enable him to destroy his enemies. But as this blood was a deadly poison, and even its effluvia might be fatal, he must prepare an antidote from the juice of a plant, which she named. On the following day he procured the plant, and his wife, who knew nothing of the fatal price he was to pay, assisted him in making the infusion. He also made a cedar arrow, and, with bow in hand, repaired to the pool.

At his call the water began to rise, boiling fearfully. As it rose, an animal came forth. It proved to be a large bird, a "diver," and the warrior said, "This is not the one," and let it go. The water boiled and rose higher, and a porcupine came out. "Neither is this the one," said the warrior, and withdrew his arrow from his bow. Then the water rose in fury to the level of the bank, and the head of a huge horned serpent, with distended jaws and flaming eyes, rose and glared at Tijaiha. "This is the one," he said, and shot the creature in the neck. The blood gushed forth, and he caught in a vessel, which he held ready, about half a pint.

Then he ran toward his lodge, but before he reached it he had become nearly blind and all but helpless. His wife put the kettle to his lips. He drank the antidote, and presently vomited the black poison, and regained his strength. In the morning he called to his wife's mother, but she was dead. She had perished without a touch from a human hand. In this manner he became possessed of a talisman which, as he believed, would give him a charmed life, and secure him the victory over his enemies.

But in some way it became known that he had been the cause of the mother's death. This crime excited the indignation of his people, and he dared not go back to them. He took refuge with the Iroquois, and became a noted war-chief among them.

After some time he resolved, in an evil hour, to lead an attack against his own people. He set forth at the head of a strong party of warriors, and arrived at the Wyandot (Huron) settlement, near the present town of Sandwich. It was the season of corn-planting, and two of Tijaihas aunts had come out on that day to plant their fields. They were women of high rank in the tribe, and Tijaiha knew that their death would arouse the whole tribe. He ordered his followers to kill them. This they did, and then retreated into the forest to the northward, carefully covering their tracks, to escape pursuit. Their leader's expectation was that the Huron warriors would go off in another direction in search of their enemies, thus leaving their defenseless town at his mercy.

When the Hurons found the bodies they were greatly excited. They searched for ten days without discovering any trace of the murderers. Their chief then consulted a noted soothsayer, who promised that on the following day he would tell him all. During the night the soothsayer made his incantations, and in the morning informed the Hurons that the deed had been done by a party of Iroquois, under the lead of Tijaiha. The enemy, he said, was lurking in the woods, and he could guide them to the spot; but they must wait ten days before starting.

The Hurons waited impatiently until the ten days had expired, and then placed the old soothsayer on horseback, and followed him. He led them through the forest directly to the encampment of their enemies. On seeing them they waited till evening, and then through the night, till daybreak. Then, according to their custom, they shouted to their sleeping foes, and rushed upon them. They killed every man in the camp; but on examining carefully the bodies, they were annoyed to find that Tijaiha was not among them.

Being hungry, they seated themselves to eat, and the chief, feeling thirsty, told his son to take his kettle and bring him some water. "Where shall I find water here?" asked the boy.

"These men must have had water," replied his father. "Look for the path they have made to it." The lad looked, and found the path, and, following it, came to a deep spring or pool under a tree.

As he was stooping down to it a man rose partly out of the pool, and bade the youth take him prisoner. The affrighted boy ran to the camp and told what he had seen. All shouted "Tijaiha," and rushed to the pool, where they dragged him forth by the hair.

He stood defiant and sneering, while they attempted to kill him. Their blows seemed powerless to injure him. He caught the tomahawks that were aimed at him, and hurled them back. At length a warrior, exclaiming, "I will finish him," plunged a knife into his breast and tore out his heart. Thrown on the ground, it bounded like a living thing, till the warrior split it open with his knife. Thus ended Tijaiha's evil career. His contract with the serpent had only led him to crime and death.

Source: Adapted from Hale, Horatio. "Huron Folklore II: The Story of Tihaiha, the Sorceror," *Journal of American Folklore,* 2 (1889): 249–54, pp. 250–52.

Witch Men from Acoma

The pueblos mentioned in this tale are located in agricultural villages in New Mexico. Acoma and Laguna are linguistically and culturally similar, while Zuni is much further west and dissimilar in both language and culture. Witches in these cultures could be of either gender and were noted by their ability to "shape-shift," to exchange their human forms for animal shapes (particularly coyote or owl) in order to work their mischief anonymously.

A long time ago two men left the pueblo of Acoma to see a Laguna dance. They were on burros. There were no horses then. As they came along they saw two men walking ahead of them. When they reached them they recognized them. They were also from Acoma. They belonged to the witch society. They were walking.

"Where are you going?" said the first two.

"We are going to Laguna," said the witch men.

"When will you get to Laguna?"

"We expect to get there by evening," replied the first two men.

"We are only walking but we will get there before you do," said the witch men. "We will get there by noon."

The other two said nothing more. They went ahead on their burros and left the witch men behind. "Those two are witches," said one of them. "I am afraid of them. Did you hear them say that they would be in Laguna by noon? They are certainly witches. We must be careful."

After a while they turned around and saw two coyotes running behind them. The witch men had turned into coyotes by going through a hoop. They caught up with the men and passed them. As they passed them one of the coyotes was heard saying to the other in a low voice, "We are on foot and they are on burros and we can travel faster."

"Surely those two coyotes are our Acoma friends," said one of the men to the other. "They have become coyotes to do us some harm."

The coyotes soon disappeared ahead of them, but in a short while they appeared again coming back. They met the two Acoma men and passed them. As they passed one of them called out, "Well, you are still here, are you? You don't seem to go very fast on your burros?"

They disappeared. Soon one of the men turned back and saw them coming after them again. "There they come again, those coyotes, the witches," he said to his companion. "If we don't look out they will surely do us some harm." This time they came running and they only howled as they passed.

The witch men arrived at Laguna. Before entering the pueblo they passed through hoops and became men again. They arrived at noon.

The other two men arrived about sunset. They were frightened. They saw the witch men there and they told everybody about what had happened on the road. The two witch men said they knew nothing about it. But the other two were sure they were the men and coyotes they had seen on the road. The witch men were very handsome fellows.

The next day they saw a very pretty Laguna girl and they planned to steal her. They wanted to take her to their witch cave in the Enchanted Mesa. They courted the girl and arranged to meet her at the river at sundown.

At sundown the next day the witch men met the Laguna girl at the river when she went down for water. They asked her if she wanted to go to Acoma with them. She said she would ask her father. "But your father will not let you go," they said.

"Then I will not go," said the girl. They began to use their witch powers over her and one of them put her to sleep. When she was asleep they put her through a hoop and she became a coyote. Then they also went through hoops and became coyotes. Then they awoke the girl and all three started for Acoma in the form of coyotes. The girl walked between the two. They did not go by the straight road, but over the hills and cliffs as coyotes go. And since she was now a coyote she did not know what had happened to her. Soon they reached the witch cave of the Enchanted Mesa. There they prepared a bed of pelts for her. They put her through a hoop and she became the beautiful girl that she was. They also became men again. They asked her if she knew where she was. She did not know. They put her to sleep with their magic powers. They made a fire and sat by her side watching.

At the Laguna pueblo the parents of the girl became worried when the girl did not return with her water jar. They began to ask about her. A little boy said he had seen the two witch men talking to her. They looked for them all over the village, but could not find them anywhere. They went to the river and there they found the water jar left by the girl. The two men from Acoma again told their story and everybody suspected the witch men. The men of Laguna met and four men were selected to go with the two Acoma men to hunt for the witch men and the girl.

They started at once armed with bows and arrows. One of them was a magician Soon after they started the magician ordered a halt and he had a fire built. He threw some magic powders in the fire. A blue flame came out. Then he said, "I know all about it now. The two witch men from Acoma that came to Laguna have stolen the girl. We must hurry. I am not afraid of witches. I have fought with them before."

When they came near the Enchanted Mesa the magician said to the others, "Listen to that bird singing. It is warning us of danger. We are near the witch men." Then they began to climb the mesa.

The witch men heard them going up. They left the girl in the cave asleep. They became coyotes and ran around and back of the mesa. There they became men and began to attack their pursuers with poisoned arrows. They were too far away and could not hit them.

While they were fighting, the magician and the two Acoma men went up to the cave and rescued the girl. The magician made her awaken. He asked her if she knew where she was. She did not know. She did not remember anything. They took her with them and immediately left for Laguna. The other three men kept on fighting with the witches.

Finally, the witch men went back to the cave to get more poisoned arrows. When they arrived they did not find the girl. They were very angry. With many arrows they started back to fight their enemies. The three men were already near Laguna. The witch men hid their arrows under their skin and came up to them and began to talk with them in a friendly manner. "We are looking for some burros we lost." As one of them turned around one of the men shot an arrow into his back.

"There is one of your burros, you witch," he said to him. The other one went through a hoop and became a coyote. He started to run away. As he ran he was shot in the leg with an arrow, but he disappeared in the darkness.

The other one was caught. "I am bleeding too much and I must lie down and rest," he said. They decided to sleep there and go to Laguna the next day. During the night while the others were sleeping he too became a coyote and ran away. But when they awakened they followed the trail of blood and caught him. Then they made a fire to burn him. They burned him first on one side and then on the other.

When they were burning him he exclaimed, "Why do you burn me when I am a man like you?"

"But you are a witch, and we must burn you," they replied. They burned him to ashes.

The other witch man reached Acoma by morning. But he knew all would recognize him by the wound in the leg. He did not enter the village. He decided to go to Zuni to live. And no one has ever heard of him again. And the girl was taken safely to her parents at Laguna.

Source: Adapted from "Pueblo Indian Folk Tales," Aurelio M. Espinosa, *Journal of American Folklore,* 49 (1936): 69–133, pp. 75–77.

The Raven Mocker

According to traditional medical theories of the Cherokee of the southeastern United States, death is due to a personal attack. This attack may come from a nonhuman, supernatural source, or from a human agent such as a witch. The witch, as is the case in many other traditions, carries out his or her mischief under cover of darkness. Therefore, the Cherokee term for witch translates as "nightgoer."

Of all the Cherokee wizards or witches the most dreaded is the Raven Mocker, the one that robs the dying man of life. They are of either sex and there is no sure way to know one, though they usually look withered and old, because they have added so many lives to their own.

At night, when some one is sick or dying in the settlement, the Raven Mocker goes to the place to take the life. He flies through the air in fiery shape, with arms outstretched like wings, and sparks trailing behind, and a rushing sound like the noise of a strong wind. Every little while as he flies he makes a cry like the cry of a raven when it "dives" in the air—not like the common raven cry—and those who hear are afraid, because they know that some man's life will soon go out. When the Raven Mocker comes to the house he finds others of his kind waiting there, and unless there is a doctor on guard who knows how to drive them away they go inside, all invisible, and frighten and torment the sick man until they kill him. Sometimes, to do this, they even lift him from the bed and throw him on the floor, but his friends who are with him think he is only struggling for breath.

After the witches kill him they take out his heart and eat it, and so add to their own lives as many days or years as they have taken from his. No one in the room can see them, and there is no sear where they take out the heart, but yet there is no heart left in the body. Only one who has the right medicine can recognize a Raven Mocker, and if such a man stays in the room with the sick person these witches are afraid to come in, and retreat as soon as they see him, because when one of them is recognized in his right shape he must die within seven days. There was once a man who had this medicine and used to hunt for Raven Mockers, and killed several. When the friends of a dying person know that there is no more hope they always try to have one of these medicine men stay in the house and watch the body until it is buried, because after burial the witches do not steal the heart.

The other witches are jealous of the Raven Mockers and afraid to come into the same house with one. Once a man, who had the witch medicine, was watching by a sick man and saw these other witches outside trying to get in. All at once they heard a Raven Mocker cry overhead and the others scattered "like a flock of pigeons when the hawk swoops." When at last a Raven Mocker dies these other witches sometimes take revenge by digging up the body and abusing it.

The following is told on the reservation as an actual happening:

A young man had been out on a hunting trip and was on his way home when night came on while he was still a long distance from the settlement. He knew of a house not far off the trail where an old man and his wife lived, so he turned in that direction to look for a place to sleep until morning. When he got to the house there was nobody in it. He looked into the sweat lodge and found no one there either. He thought maybe they had gone after water, and so stretched himself out in the farther corner to sleep. Very soon he heard a raven cry outside, and in a little while afterwards the old man came into the sweat lodge and sat down by the fire without noticing the young man, who kept still in the dark corner. Soon there was another raven cry outside, and the old man said to himself, "Now my wife is coming," and sure enough in a little while the old woman came in and sat down by her husband. Then the young man knew they were Raven Mockers and he was frightened and kept very quiet.

Said the old man to his wife, "Well, what luck did you have?" "None," said the old woman, "there were too many doctors watching. What luck did you have?" "I got what I went for," said the old man, "there is no reason to fail, but you never have luck. Take this and cook it and let's have something to eat." She fixed the fire and then the young man smelled meat roasting and thought it smelled sweeter than any meat he had ever tasted. He peeped out from one eye, and it looked like a man's heart roasting on a stick.

Suddenly the old woman said to her husband, "Who is over in the corner?" "Nobody," said the old man. "Yes, there is," said the old woman, "I hear him snoring," and she stirred the fire until it blazed and lighted up the whole place, and there was the young man lying in the corner. He kept quiet and pretended to be asleep. The old man made a noise at the fire to wake him, but still he pretended to sleep. Then the old man came over and shook him, and he sat up and rubbed his eyes as if he had been asleep all the time.

Now it was near daylight and the old woman was out in the other house getting breakfast ready, but the hunter could hear her crying to herself. "Why is your wife crying?" he asked the old man. "Oh, she has lost some of her friends lately and feels lonesome," said her husband; but the young man knew that she was crying because he had heard them talking.

When they came out to breakfast the old man put a bowl of corn mush before him and said, "This is all we have—we have had no meat for a long time." After breakfast the young man started on again, but when he had gone a little way the old man ran after him with a fine piece of bead work and gave it to him, saying, "Take this, and don't tell anybody what you heard last, night, because my wife and I are always quarreling that way." The young man took the piece, but when he came to the first creek he threw it into the water and then went on to the settlement. There he told the whole story, and a party of warriors started back with him to kill the Raven Mockers. When they reached the place it was seven days after the first night. They found the old man and his wife lying dead in the house, so they set fire to it and burned it and the witches together.

Source: Adapted from "The Raven Mocker," James Mooney. *Myths of the Cherokee*. From Nineteenth Annual Report of the Bureau of American Ethnology 1897-98, Part I. [1900]. (Washington, D.C: U.S. Government Printing Office, 1900), pp. 401–3

The Skin-Shifting Old Woman

The following supernatural narrative focuses on Wichita sorcery. Traditionally, the Wichita followed a semi-sedentary lifestyle supported by gardening and a seasonal buffalo hunt. As "The Skin-Shifting Old Woman" illustrates, persons with extraordinary supernatural powers could use their magic for either good or evil. The motivation of the old woman of the tale, envy, is a common explanation for witchcraft. This tale is an especially good example of the virtually universal tendency of Native American cultures to base the plots of their narratives on patterns of fours, for example, the four trips to gather wood.

In the story of Healthy-Flint-Stone-Man, it is told that he was a powerful man and lived in a village and was a chief of the place. He was not a man of heavy build, but was slim. Often when a man is of this type of build he is called "Healthy-Flint-Stone-Man," after the man in the story. Healthy-Flint-Stone-Man had parents, but at this time he had no wife. Soon afterwards he married, and his wife was the prettiest woman that ever lived in the village. When she married Healthy-Flint-Stone-Man they lived at his home. She was liked by his parents, for she was a good worker and kind-hearted. As was their custom, the men of the village came at night to visit Healthy-Flint-Stone-Man, and his wife did the cooking to feed them, so that he liked her all the more, and was kind to her.

Early one morning a strange woman by the name of Little-Old-Woman came to their place and asked the wife to go with her to get wood. Out of kindness to Little-Old-Woman she went with her, leaving her husband at home. Little-Old-Woman said she knew where all the dry wood was to be found. When they reached the place where she thought there was plenty of wood they did not stop. They went on past, although there was plenty of good dry wood. The wife began to cut wood for the old woman and some for herself. When she had cut enough for both she fixed it into two bundles, one for each. Little-Old-Woman knelt by her pile and waited for the wife to help her up. Little-Old-Woman then helped the wife in the same way, and they started toward their home. They talked on the way about their manner of life at home. Arrived at the village, the old woman went to her home. When the wife got home she began to do her work.

Again, the second time, the old woman came around and asked the wife to go with her to fetch wood. They started away together, and this time went farther than on the first time to get their wood, though they passed much good wood. The wife cut wood for both and arranged it in two piles, but this time she herself first knelt by her pile and asked the old woman to take hold of her hands and pull her up; then the wife helped the old woman with her load.

They returned home, and on the way the old woman said to the wife, "If you will go with me to fetch wood for the fourth time I shall need no more help from you." They again went far beyond where any other women had gone to get wood. When they got to the village they parted. The wife wondered why the old woman came to her for help. She found the men passing the time talking of the past as usual. She kept on doing her duty day after day.

The third time the old woman came for the wife to ask her to help her fetch wood, as she was all out of it again. Again they went out, and this time they went still further for the wood, and now they were getting a long way from the village. The wife cut wood and arranged it in two bundles, one for each of them to carry. This time it was the old woman's turn first to be helped up with the wood. They helped each other, and on the way home the old woman told the wife that they had only once more to go for wood, and the work would all be done. She always seemed thankful for the help she received. They reached the village and went to their homes. The wife found her men as usual, and commenced to do her work. After the men were through eating they went home, though some stayed late in the night.

Finally, the old woman came the fourth time to ask the wife to go with her and help her fetch some wood. This time they went about twice as far as they had gone the third time from the village. When the old woman thought they were far enough they stopped, and the wife began cutting wood for both of them. When she had cut enough she arranged it in two bundles. Now it was the wife's turn to be helped up with the wood, but the old woman refused to do it as usual and told her to go ahead and kneel by the bundle of wood. The wife refused. Now, each tried to persuade the other to kneel first against the bundle of wood. The old woman finally prevailed, and the wife knelt against the wood, and as she put her robe around her neck the old woman seemed pleased to help her, but as the old woman was fixing the carrying ropes she tightened them, after slipping them around the wife's neck until the wife fell at full length, as though dying.

The old woman sat down to rest, as she was tired from choking the wife. Soon she got up and untied the wife. Now, they were in the thick timber, and there was flowing water through it. After the old woman had killed the wife she blew into the top of her head and blew the skin from her, hair and all. This she did because she envied the wife her good looks, since the wife was the best-looking woman in the village, and her husband was good-looking and well thought of by all the prominent men, and the old woman wanted to be treated as well as the wife had been treated. Then the old woman began to put on the wife's skin, but the wife was a little smaller than the old woman, though the old woman managed to stretch the skin and drew it over her, fitting herself to it. Then she smoothed down the skin until it fitted her nicely. She took the wife's body to the flowing water and threw it in, having found a place that was never visited by anyone, and that had no trail leading to it. She then went to her pile of wood and took it to her home. She found the men visiting Healthy-Flint-Stone-Man.

Healthy-Flint-Stone-Man did not discover that she was not his wife. The old woman knew all about the former wife's ways, for she had talked much with her when they were coming home with the wood, and she had asked the wife all sorts of questions about her husband. She understood how the men carried on at the his place. The wife had told her husband that the old woman had said that they were to go for wood four different times, and the last time being the fourth time, he supposed it was all over and his wife had got through with the old woman. So, as the old woman was doing his wife's duty, he thought her to be his wife until the time came when the skin began to decay and the hair to come off.

Still there were big crowds of men around, and the old woman began to be fearful lest they would find her out. So she made as if she were sick. Healthy-Flint-Stone-Man tried to get a man to doctor her, but she refused to be doctored. Finally, he hired a servant to doctor her. This was the man who always sat right by the entrance, ready to do errands or carry announcements to the people. His name was Buffalo-Crow-Man. He had a dark complexion. The old woman began to rave at his medicine working. He began to tell who the old woman was, saying that there was no need of doctoring her; that she was a fraud and an evil spirit; and that she had become the wife of Healthy-Flint-Stone-Man through her bad deeds. The old woman told her husband not to believe the servant; and that he himself was a fraud and was trying to get her to do something wrong. The servant then stood at the feet of the old woman and began to sing.

Then over her body he went and jumped at her head. Then he commenced to sing again, first on her left side, then on her right. He sang the song four times, and while he was doing this the decayed hide came off from her. The servant told the men to take her out and take her life for what she had done to Healthy-Flint-Stone-Man wife, telling how she had fooled him. They did as they were told. The servant told the men he had suspected the old woman when she had come around to get the wife to go after wood with her; that when going after wood they always went a long distance, so that no one could observe them, but that he had always taken the form of a crow and flown very high over them, so they could not see him, and had watched them; that on the fourth time they went for wood he had seen the old woman choke the wife with the wife's rope; how the old woman had secured the whole skin of the wife and had thrown her body into the flowing water. He told the men where the place was, and directed them there the next day. The men went to their homes, feeling very sad for the wicked thing the old woman had done.

On the next day Healthy-Flint-Stone-Man went as directed, and he came to a place where he found a pile of wood that belonged to his former wife. He went to the place where he supposed his wife to be. He sat down and commenced to weep. There he stayed all night and the next day. He returned to his home, but he could not forget the occurrence. So he went back again and stayed another night and again returned home. He was full of sorrow. He went back to the place the third time, and when he got there he sat down and commenced to weep. Again he stayed all night, and early next morning it was foggy and he could not see far. While he sat and wept he faced the east, and he was on the west side of the flowing waters, so that he also faced the flowing water wherein his wife's body was thrown.

He heard some one singing, but he was unable to catch the sound so that he could locate the place where the sound came from. He finally discovered that it came from the flowing water. He went toward the place and listened, and indeed it was his wife's voice, and this is what she sang:

> Woman-having-Powers-in-the-Water,
> Woman-having-Powers-in-the-Water,
> I am the one (you seek),
> I am here in the water.

As he went near the river he saw in the middle of the water his wife standing on the water. She told him to go back home and tell his parents to clean their grass-lodge and to purify the room by burning sage. She told her husband that he might then return and take her home; that he should tell his parents not to weep when she should return, but that they should rejoice at her return to life, and that after that he could take her home.

So the man started to his home. After he arrived he told his mother to clean and purify the lodge; and that he had found his wife and that he was going back again to get her. He told her that neither she nor any of their friends should weep at the sight of the woman. While his mother was doing this cleaning he went back to the river and stayed one more night, and early in the morning he heard the woman singing again. He knew that he was to bring his wife back to his home. When he heard her sing he went straight to her. She came out of the water and he met her. She began to tell her husband about her troubles–how she met troubles and how he was deceived. That day they went to their home, and Flint-Stone-Man's parents were glad to see his wife back once more. They lived together until long afterward.

Source: Adapted from "The Skin Shifting Old Woman," *Tales of the North American Indians.* Stith Thompson (Bloomington, IN: Indiana University Press, 1929), pp. 186–190.

The Man-Eater and His Younger Brother

The bearers of this tale, the Seneca, traditionally resided in what is now western New York, subsisting by growing corn, beans, and squash; gathering wild plant foods; and hunting and fishing. The motif of the brother turning cannibal after isolation in the wilderness is reminiscent of beliefs that exist further north in Subarctic Canada. In them, isolation and, often, attack by the spirit known as the Windigo leads to an insatiable craving for human flesh. The escape by means of magical objects and supernatural helpers is a common episode in world folklore.

Two brothers went on a hunting expedition. After they had been quite a while in the woods and had good luck in finding game, they built a bark house.

At first they had everything in common, but one day the elder said to the younger, "We must live apart for the future. We will make a partition in the middle of the house and have a door at each end. You will always go out of the door in your part of the house and I will go out of the one in my part."

The younger brother agreed, and they made the partition, then the elder brother said, "Now each one will live by himself. I will not go to your part of the house and you will not come to mine. When we want to say anything we will talk through the partition. You can hunt birds and animals, but I will hunt men and kill them. Neither of us will marry or bring a woman to the house. If I marry, you will kill me if you can. If you marry, I will try to kill you."

Both agreed to this arrangement, and for a long time lived according to it, but one day, when the brothers were out hunting, a woman came to the younger brother's part of the house. The elder brother tracked her, caught her at the door, dragged her into his part of the house, killed and ate her. When the younger brother came home the elder said, "I had good luck today, near home."

The younger knew what his brother had done, but all he said was, "It is well to have good luck."

A second time the elder brother tracked a woman to his brother's part of the house. This time he knocked at the door and called out, "Give me a couple of arrows; there is an elk out here."

The woman carried him the arrows and the minute she opened the door he killed her. He dragged the body into his part of the house and ate it up. When the younger brother came, he talked through the partition as before, but said nothing about the woman.

The next woman who came to him he warned against opening the door, told her not to open it for anyone, even for him; he would come in himself.

The elder brother ran to the door, knocked and called out, "Give me a couple of arrows; there is a bear out here."

The woman sat by the fire, did not move.

Again he called, "Give me the arrows; the bear will get away."

She did not stir, and after a while he went into his own part of the house.

When the younger brother came the woman told him what had happened. While they were whispering, the elder brother called out, "Brother, you are whispering to someone. Who is it? Haven't you a woman in there?"

"I am counting my game," answered the young man. There was silence for a time, then the young man began whispering cautiously to the woman. He said, "In the morning my brother and I will have a life and death struggle. You must help me, but it will be difficult for he will make himself like me in form and voice, but strike him if you can." The woman took a small squash shell and tied it in the young man's hair so she might distinguish him.

The cannibal brother again called out, "You have a woman in there. You are whispering to her," but he got no answer.

In the morning the brothers met and began to fight with clubs and flint knives. When their weapons broke, they clinched. Soon both were on the ground. Sometimes one was under, sometimes the other. The elder brother was exactly like the younger and repeated his words. Whenever the younger called to the woman, "Strike him!" the elder cried out, "Strike him!"

The woman could not tell which one to strike. At last she caught sight of the squash shell. Then she struck a heavy blow and killed the elder brother. They put the body on a pile of wood and burned it up, then scattered the ashes.

But the young man knew his brother would come to life. He put the woman in a cattail, put the cattail on the point of his arrow and shot it far away to the West. Then he ran through the heart of the post of the house, sprang after the arrow and coming to the ground ran with great speed till he found where the arrow had struck and the cattail burst open. Then he soon overtook the woman and they traveled on together.

He said, "We must travel fast, for my brother will come to life and follow us."

The next morning they heard somebody whoop. The young man said, "That is my brother; he will destroy us if he can."

He changed the woman into a half-decayed stump; hid himself a short distance away, and, taking off his moccasins, told them to run on ahead; to go quickly through swamps and thickets and over hills and mountains and come back to him by a roundabout way.

When the elder brother reached the rotten stump, he looked at it and was suspicious but he followed the moccasins and went on swiftly all day and all night, then he turned back. When he came to the place where he had seen the stump, and it was not there, he was awfully angry, for he knew he had been fooled. He found his brother's tracks and followed them.

When they heard him whoop, the young man took out of his pouch the jaw of a beaver, stuck the teeth in the ground, and said, "Let beavers come and build a dam across the world so water may rise to my brother's neck, and let the beavers bite him when he tries to cross the dam."

When the elder brother came up, the dam was built, and the water was neck high; his brother's tracks disappeared at the edge of the water, and he said, "If they have gone through, I can."

When the water reached his breast, beavers began to bite him. He was forced to turn back and look for another crossing. He ran all day, but could find no end to the dam. Then he cried out, "I have never heard that there was a beaver dam across the world," and turning he ran back to the place he had started from. The dam was gone, all that remained was a beaver's jaw with two teeth in it.

The man-eater hurried along as fast as he could and again the man and woman heard his whoop. The man took a pigeon-feather from his pouch, placed it on the ground, and said, "Let all the pigeons in the world come and leave droppings here." All the pigeons in the world came and soon there was a ridge six feet high, made of droppings.

When the elder brother came to the ridge, he said, "Their tracks are here; if they have gone through, I can."

He tried, and when he could not get through he turned back and ran eastward to look for an opening, ran all day. The ridge was everywhere. He went back to the place that he had started from and slept till morning. When he wakened, the ridge was gone; all he found was a pigeon feather sticking in the ground.

After dropping the feather, the younger brother and the woman ran till they came to where an old man sat mending a fish net.

The old man said, "I will delay the man-eater as long as I can. You have an aunt living west of here, beyond her house the trail passes between two rocks that move backward and forward so quickly that whoever tries to go between them is crushed, but beg of your aunt and she will stop them."

The two hurried on, came to the woman and begged her to help them. She stopped the rocks long enough for them to spring through, then she said,

"You will soon reach a river. On the other side of the river you will see a man with a canoe, beckon to him and he will come and take you across. Beyond the river are the Frost people, but they will not harm you. A little animal will come to meet you. Follow it and it will lead you to an opening. In the opening you will find your mother's house."

When the elder brother came to the old man, who was mending a fish net, he pushed him, and called out, "Did anyone pass here?"

The old man did not answer.

He struck him a blow on the head and asked again, "Did anyone pass here?"

The fisherman threw his net over the man, entangled him and he fell, but after struggling a time he freed himself and hurried on. When he came to the woman who guarded the rocks he begged her to stop them and let him pass. She refused and he watched for a chance to spring through. At last, when he thought the rocks were moving slowly, he jumped. He was caught and half his body was crushed; but he rubbed it with saliva and cured it. Then he hurried on. When he came to the river and saw the man on the opposite bank he shouted to him to come with his canoe and take him across, but the man did not look up. He shouted again and got no answer, then he swam across.

On that side of the river was a forest where all of the trees had been stripped of bark and killed by the hammering of mud-turtle rattles. The hammering had been done by the Frost people in keeping time while they danced. These people turned upon the man-eater, killed him, hammered all the flesh off his body, then hammered his bones till there was not a bit of them left.

When the mother saw her son and his wife, she was happy and said, "I am glad that you have come. I was afraid that your brother, who stole you away from me, would kill you. Now you will stay with me always."

Source: Adapted from "The Man-Eater and His Brother," *Seneca Indian Myths.* Jeremiah Curtin (New York: E.P. Dutton and Company, 1922), pp. 369–373.

A Journey to the Land of the Skeletons

The following narrative told by the Hopi addresses the universal human need to comprehend the afterlife. The tale also serves particular Hopi ends. The concerns of an agricultural people are reflected in the role of the spirits in bringing rainfall and the codes of behavior required to attain a tranquil existence in the land of the dead characterize the groups social norms.

In Shongópavi, the Hopi village where the people were living first, there a young man was often sitting at the edge of the village looking at the graveyards and wondering what became of the dead, whether it is true that they continue to live somewhere. He spoke to his father about it. His father could not tell him very much.

"We do not know much about it," he said; "so, that is what you are thinking about." His father was the village chief. He said to his son that he would speak to the other chiefs and to his assistants about it, which he did. He talked about it especially to the village crier, and told them that those were the things that his son was thinking about, and whether they knew anything about it.

"Yes," they said, The Badger Old Man has the medicine for it and knows about it. We shall inform him." So they called the Badger Old Man. When he arrived he asked them what they wanted with him. "Yes," they said, "this young man is thinking about these dead, whether they live anywhere, and you know about it, you have medicine for that, and that is the reason why we called you."

"Very well," he said, "so, that is why you wanted me. I shall go and get my medicine."

So he went over to his house and looked over his medicines and finally found the right one. "This is the medicine," he said, and took it, returning to the village. "Very well," he said; "now when does he want to find out about it?"

"Tomorrow," they said. "Very well; have you a white kilt?"

"Yes," the village chief replied. "You put this on your son the next morning," he said, "and then you blacken his chin with black shale, and tie a small eagle feather to his forehead." The next morning they dressed up the young Man as they were instructed, preparing him as they prepare the dead. Hereupon the Badger Old Man spread a white blanket on the floor and told the young man to lie down on it. He then placed some medicine into his mouth, which the young man ate. He also placed some medicine into his ears and some on his heart. Then he wrapped him up in a robe, whereupon the young man, after moving a little, "died." "This is the medicine," the Badger Old Man said, "if he eats this he will go far away and then come back again. He wanted to see something and find out something, and with this medicine he will find out."

After the young man had fallen asleep he saw a path leading westward. It was the road to the Skeleton house. This road he followed and after a while he met someone who was sitting there.

"What have you come for?" he asked the young man.

"Yes," he replied, "I have come to find out about your life here."

"Yes," the other one replied, "I did not follow the straight road; I did not listen, and I now have to wait here. After a certain number of days I can go on a little, then I can go on again, but it will be a long time before I shall get to Skeleton house." This one was simply living in an enclosure of sticks. That was all the house and protection he had.

From here the young man proceeded westward. The path led through large cactus and through many agave plants so that sometimes the trail could hardly be distinguished. He finally arrived at the rim of a steep bluff. Here somebody was sitting. He asked the young man why he had come, and the latter told him.

"Very well," the chief said. "Away over there is the house that you are going to," but as there was a great deal of smoke in the distance the young man could not see the house. But hereupon the chief placed the young man's kilt on the ground, placed the young man on it, then lifted it up, and holding it over the precipice he threw it forward, whereupon the young man was slowly descending on the kilt as if he were flying with wings.

When he had arrived on the ground below the bluff he put on his kilt again and proceeded. In the distance he saw a column of smoke rising from the ground. After he had proceeded a distance he came upon Skeleton Woman. He asked her what that was.

"Yes," she said, "some of those who had been wicked while living in the village were thrown in there. There is a chief there who tells them to go over this road, and throws them in there. Those who are thrown in there are destroyed, they no longer exist. You must not go there," she added, "but you keep on this road and go straight ahead toward Skeleton house."

When he arrived there he could not see any one at first except a few children who were playing there. "Oh!" they said, "here a Skeleton has come."

There was a very large village there, so he went in and now the people or Skeletons living there heard about him.

So they assembled there on all sides and looked at him. "Who are you?" they asked the young man.

"I am the village chief's son. I came from Shongópavi."

So they pointed him to the Bear clan, saying, "Those are the people that you want to see. They are your people." Because there were a great many different clans there. They are sleeping there in the daytime. So the Skeleton took him over to the house where his clan lived. "Here your ancestors are," they told him, and showed him the ladder that led up to the house, but the rungs of the ladder were made of sunflower stems. He tried to go up but the first rung broke as soon as he stepped on it, but when the Skeletons went up and down the ladder the rungs did not break. So he was wondering how he should get up.

"I shall stay down here," he said; "I shall not go up. You bring me food here and feed me down here," he said to them. So the Skeletons brought him some food.

When they saw him eat they laughed at him, because they never eat the food, but only the odor or the soul of the food. That is the reason why they are not heavy. And that is the reason why the clouds into which the dead are transformed are not heavy and can float in the air. The food itself the Skeletons threw out behind the houses. So this young man, when he was wandering around there, would sometimes eat of it. When he had eaten they asked him what he had come for.

"Yes," he said, "I was always thinking whether Skeletons live somewhere. I spoke to my father about it and told him that I wanted to go and find out whether they were staying somewhere, and my father was willing and he dressed me up in this way, and the Badger Old Man gave me some medicine that knows about this so that I could go and find out."

"So that is what you have come for; so that is why you have come here. Now, you look at us. Yes, we are thus." Thus they spoke to him, and then added, "This is the way we are living here. It is not light here; it is not as light as where you live. We are living poorly here. You must go back again, you cannot stay with us here yet; your flesh is still strong and 'salty.' you eat food yet; we only eat the odor of the food. Now you must work there for us. Make prayer feathers for us at the Soyál ceremony. These we tie around our foreheads and they represent dropping rain. We then shall work for you here, too. We shall send you rain and crops. You must wrap up the women when they die, in bridal robes, and tie the big knotted belt around them, because these robes are not tightly woven and when the Skeletons move along on them through the sky as clouds, the thin rain drops through these robes and the big raindrops fall from the fringes of the big belt. Sometimes you cannot see the clouds very distinctly because they are hidden behind these nakwákwosis just as our faces are hidden behind them."

Looking around, the young man saw some of the Skeletons walking around with big burdens on their backs, consisting of grinding stones, which they carried over their forehead by a thin string that had cut deeply into the skin. Others carried bundles of cactus on their backs, and, as they had no clothes on, the thorns of the cactus would hurt them. They were submitted to these punishments for a certain length of time, when they were relieved of them and then lived with the other people there. At another place in the Skeleton house he saw the chiefs who had been good here in this world and had made a good road for other people. They had taken their sacred bundles with them and set them up there, and when the people here in the villages have their ceremonies and smoke during the ceremonies, this smoke goes down into the other world to the sacred bundles or mothers and from there rises up in the form of clouds.

After the young man had seen everything at this place he returned. When he arrived at the steep bluff he again mounted his kilt and a slight breeze at once lifted him up. The chief, who was living here at the top of the bluff and who had assisted the young man in getting down, was a spirit. He had a big horn for a head-dress.

This chief told him that he should return now. "You have now seen how they live here; it is not good, It is not light here; no one should desire to come here. Your father and mother are mourning for you now, so you return home."

On his way back nothing happened to him and he did not meet anybody. When he had just about arrived at his house, his body, which was still lying under the covering in the room where he had fallen asleep, began to move and as he entered his body he came to life again. They removed the covering, the Badger Old Man wiped his body, washed off the paint from his face, discharmed him, and then he sat up. They fed him and then asked him what he had found out.

"Yes," he said, "because I wanted to find out this, you dressed me up and laid me down here. Then you fed me something and put some medicine on my heart. After I had died I traveled westward, and when I was traveling I came upon a woman." Then he told them of the many things he had seen.

"It is really true that the Skeletons are living somewhere, and I also saw that those who are bad here and wicked are punished there. They have to carry heavy burdens. Some carry grinding stones, and others cactus, the thorns of which prick them. Especially are those punished there in the other world that are bad to the maidens and women here. I have seen it all myself now, and I shall after this remember that and think that we are living in the light here. They are not living in the light there. So I shall not want to be thinking about that place, and no one should desire to go there, because here we are living better—we are living in the light here. I have seen it myself, and we should not think about that world so much."

"Very well," all who were sitting around said , "very well; so that is the way." Badger Old Man said to the young man: "Now you must not think about that any more. You must go home now and live there strong. Do not think about these things any more."

Source: Adapted from "Origin Myth," *Traditions of the Hopi*. H.R. Voth (Chicago: Field Columbian Museum, 1905), pp. 114–119.n

Select Bibliography

Beck, Horace. *Gluskap the Liar and Other Indian Tales.* Freeport, ME: Bond Wheelright, 1966.

Bruchac, Joseph. *Return of the Sun: Native American Tales from the Northeast Woodlands.* Berkeley, CA: Crossing Press, 1990.

Curtin, Jeremiah. *Seneca Indian Myths.* New York: W.P. Dutton, 1922; repr., New York: Dover, 2001.

Erdoes, Richard and Alfonso Ortiz. *American Indian Myths and Legends.* New York: Pantheon, 1984.

Kroeber, Karl. *Artistry in Native American Myths.* Lincoln: University of Nebraska Press, 1998.

Leeming, David and Jake Page. *Myths, Legends, and Folktales of America.* New York: Oxford University Press, 2000.

Mooney, James. *Myths of the Cherokee.* Nineteenth Annual Report of the Bureau of American Ethnology 1897–98, Part I. Washington, D.C.: United States Government Printing Office, 1900.

Stith, Thompson. *Tales of the North American Indians.* Bloomington: Indiana University Press, 1929.

Swann, Bryan. *Voices from Four Directions: Contemporary Translations of the Native Literatures of North America.* Lincoln: University of Nebraska, 2004.

Swanton, John Reed. *Myths and Tales of the Southeastern Indians.* Norman: University of Oklahoma Press, 2000.

Wiget, Andrew. *Critical Essays on Native American Literature.* Boston: G.K. Hall, 1985.

Williams, Mentor L., ed. *Schoolcraft's Indian Legends.* East Lansing: Michigan State University Press, 1956.

Index

About the Author

THOMAS A. GREEN is Associate Professor of Anthropology at Texas A&M University. His many books include *The Greenwood Library of American Folktales* (2006), and *The Greenwood Library of World Folktales* (2008).

**Sidney Silverman Library
and Learning Resource Center
Bergen Community College
400 Paramus Road
Paramus, NJ 07652-1595**

www.bergen.edu

Return Postage Guaranteed